Growing up all alone

Growing up all alone

Teenagers' Suicide

Rhonda Marie

NORTHWESTERN PUBLISHING HOUSE
Milwaukee, Wisconsin

Cover: photograph by David Kreider,
design by NPH artist Duane Weaver.

Scripture taken from
the Holy Bible, New International Version.
Copyright © 1973, 1978, 1984, International Bible Society.
Used by permission of Zondervan Bible Publishers.

Library of Congress Card 86-61504
Northwestern Publishing House
1250 N. 113th St., P.O. Box 26975, Milwaukee, WI 53226-0975
© 1986 by Northwestern Publishing House.
Published 1986
Printed in the United States of America
ISBN 0-8100-0244-2

CONTENTS

One:
Brief History of Suicide

"Did you know she made homecoming court?" "He was our star basketball player." "Everyone liked them!" "She was a straight 'A' student." "Didn't he just get a new car?" "I think I saw them both in church on Sunday." "I can't believe they're both dead."

All these comments have been made about teenagers who have taken their own lives. Suicide is the second leading cause of death among American teenagers. It's particularly tragic because no one expects teenagers, who have everything to live for, to die. Teenagers today have some of the finest educational opportunities available to them. They live in an affluent society which offers luxuries and experiences beyond their wildest dreams. Mobility is for almost anyone. Teenagers, literally, have everything they could ever want or choose at their disposal. Why then are so many of them choosing to die?

A great deal of study has gone into uncovering reasons or causes of teenage suicides. Papers and books have been written on the subject. However few can be found that deal with suicide from a Christian perspective. Statistics show that Christians are not exempt from attempting suicide or succeeding. While their faith makes them less likely to commit suicide, still Christians are not immune from using suicide in an attempt to solve their problems.

It is therefore important for Christians to learn more about suicide. It touches the lives of our teenagers, so we need to be aware of and ready to deal with it. Christians need to care about teenagers and to help prevent teenage suicide. During the past few years the study of suicide has made some remarkable advances, especially about teenage suicide. One important discovery is that there seem to be four types of suicide.

(1) *Egoistic suicide* occurs when a person no longer finds a basis for existence in life. This type is found among people who feel alienated from society. They have few community ties. They most likely suffer from loneliness and isolation. Most suicides in America fall into this category.

(2) *Altruistic suicide* is dedicated to a cause. This type is considered to be honorable or even heroic. Japanese kamikaze pilots in World War II intentionally crashed their planes and killed themselves. Their country honored these pilots for heroism. Protesters who burn themselves to death for a cause also fall under this category. Some place a soldier falling on a live grenade in this category. There are theologians who consider Samson's death to be altruistic suicide.

(3) *Anomic suicide* is a fairly recent discovery and category. It occurs when a great change takes place in

a person's family relationships, career, health or another important aspect of life. A sudden loss through death, divorce, estrangement or even a lover's quarrel might cause this type of suicide. Anomic means normless. Surprisingly even a change for the better can cause a person to attempt suicide. For example, a person suddenly becomes wealthy or an Olympic champion feels there is nothing left to win.

(3) *Fatalistic suicide* occurs almost entirely among prisoners, slaves or others who are forced to live in excessively regulated situations.

Teenage suicides almost always fall within the anomic type. Teenagers today are living in a normless society. It has been described as accelerated, mobile and compact. Just thinking about those three words in the same sentence can bring alarm.

Why has our society become anomic? The greatest factor has been the change in our value system. The value of the family has come into question. It is no longer important for a family to have both a father and a mother. It is interesting to note the increase in teenage suicide directly parallels the increased divorce rate. Two-career families have caused some disorientations of society. With both parents working, teenagers have lost a great deal of family support.

The greatest change in values revolves around the fact that religion has lost it's hold on society. Religion is no longer considered to be in the mainstream of life for the family. Society has become too busy for religion, and in many cases religion has become too busy for society.

With this loss of religious values comes the loss of religious support. The Christian community where a teenager could come for support and encouragement is no longer available. The pastor-as-counselor role is soon forgotten by teenagers out of contact with the church.

When society loses the value of religion, it also loses the value of moral living. The result is immorality. All the things contrary to religious values take over — murder, robbery, theft, fornication and so many more. The religious sanctity of marriage is buried in adultery. There is lack of commitment and caring between marriage partners. The children born to these couples feel this lack profoundly. The loss of religious values and decline of morals can be seen and felt in our society today. Why it has become extremely difficult to live in for teenagers we can discover as we look into the characteristics and needs of adolescents in general.

Adolescence is an escalation stage in every sense of the word. An adolescent is too young to drive the car whenever he or she would like and too old to cry and pout when not allowed to have the car. Adolescence has been described as feeling like somone is stepping on the gas pedal and the brake pedal at the same time.

It's true everyone has to go through adolescence. For the most part people have made it through, too. However today's adolescents have additional pains and problems adults need to be aware of. These have been explained by the parent of a teenage suicide victim. "Their traumas," he said, "are not what ours were when we were growing up."

It's hard to understand the difference, but the difference is there and needs to be recognized. Teenagers are facing a society today with many of the supports pulled out from under them. Christians aware of this can be of immense help to teenagers. There is need for strong Christian witness and example, a return to

Christian values and morals. The family needs to be strengthened and brought back together. Teenagers need caring adults to show them who they are and where they are going.

Teenagers need adults to tell them the pains and problems of adolescence really do pass. What hurts one day will not necessarily hurt tomorrow or next week or next year. This fact is the key (if there can be a key) to teenage suicide prevention. The pain will pass.

The fact that the pain will pass also gives concerned parents and adults hope concerning teenage suicide attempts. If a teenager can be supported during his or her crisis period, suicidal thoughts and tendencies will pass too. Case upon case of teenage suicide attempts have been recorded. Counselors and physicians can verify the number of teenagers who have been successfully helped through their traumas. These teenagers are today successful, happy and well-adjusted adults.

It is also important for adults to share this fact with teenagers. Virtually everyone has had thoughts of suicide at some time or another. People who think about suicide are not necessarily crazy or mentally ill. Suicidal thoughts need to be talked about with adults who care and can help. Adults on the other hand have a responsibility to know and learn more about suicide. If suicide is not an act of an insane or mentally ill person, what is it? Why do people commit suicide? Why are teenagers attempting suicide? The first thing to know and make others aware of is the fact that a suicide attempt is actually a cry for help. Most people who attempt suicide do not desire to die. They hope and even plan to be stopped and helped.

The father of psychiatry, Sigmund Freud, tried to explain suicide in terms of depression. Depression originates from anger toward a love object, Freud thought. People who cannot express anger turn it back on themselves. Freud pictured suicide as a kind of inverted murder. Freud did not consider social structures as an important cause of suicide.

6   Emile Durkheim wrote *Suicide* in 1897 and added to Freud's evaluation of suicide causes. He explained that people are prone to suicide when they are not part of any religious, communal or family group. He felt people were more prone to suicide when they suffered some disruption in their social structure.

Most suicide studies since are a mixture of Freud and Durkheim. Psychiatrists and psychologists today believe that psychosocial circumstance and personal tragedy together form the basis for suicide, attempted or actual.

In 1936 Karl Menninger wrote a book titled *Man against Himself.* In it he stated he found some definite connections between suicide and other self-destructive behaviors such as alcoholism, drug addiction, etc. We have already learned that almost everyone thinks about suicide. Menninger went one step further in explaining how human beings most often attempt suicide. They simply use less visible means and techniques. Menninger backed up his theory about suicide by narrowing it down to three motives: 1) the wish to kill, 2) the wish to be killed, 3) the wish to die.

The wish to kill motivates one person to kill another. Menninger explains that a person who kills is filled with self-hatred. In killing another the person expresses a desire to kill him or herself.

The wish to be killed motivates one person to shoot at another person in a conscious or unconscious effort to be shot and killed. It motivates daredevils to attempt death-defying feats. It motivates people to drink too much or eat too much when they know it is unhealthy for them. Someone who smokes excessively knowing it causes health problems is motivated by the wish to be killed.

The wish to die motivates a person to actually try to kill him or herself. A direct and deliberate suicide attempt. But it may be called accidental when reporting what happened to the car or motorcycle.

Teenage suicide could have any of these three motives. We have teenagers who have killed another person. We have teenagers who display self-destructive behavior such as drinking too much or driving too fast. And we have teenagers who deliberately try to take their own lives. We hear and read about them in the news every day. What can concerned Christians do to help? What do we need to know?

We cannot deal here with all the problems and self-destructive behaviors present in our society. However in dealing with teenage suicide we will be touching other areas. The problem of teenage suicide is so difficult to narrow down because it encompasses every aspect of life. We will be able to see this as we look at what type of a teenager or young adult might be expected to attempt suicide. Almost any teenager could be a likely candidate for suicide.

Studies to date show the highest rate of suicide among college students. College students feel tremendous pressures to achieve. These pressures could be real or imagined. The student's parents or guardians could be placing certain pressures on the student to achieve. They are real. Or the student could feel he or she is being pressured when pressure is not really there, but imagined.

Pressure, real or imagined, has caused students to commit suicide. College students feel a responsibility to succeed, and the thought of failure is so devastating to them that they will face death rather than failure. Some students feel that if they fail they will lose parental love. This, again, can be real or imagined, but it can still cause a student to commit suicide.

8   A college student feeling immense pressure to succeed spends a great deal of time studying. Study habits that cause a person to continually separate from other people are dangerous. People who study all the time put up barriers to guard them from other people. At some point they actually become afraid of being with people. They develop what psychologists call antisocial behavior.

When antisocial behavior is present, suicidal thoughts occur. The person begins to feel alone in the world and soon concludes that no one loves him or her or even cares if he or she committed suicide. It happens quickly. College students have seen their friends develop antisocial behavior and then become suicidal. Most did not know how serious the situation was.

Teenagers often decide to attend college to escape the pressures of family and friends. They may find that once in college they become lonesome for family and friends. These lonesome feelings could also trigger antisocial behavior and suicidal thoughts.

A college student may be able to handle the pressure to succeed. He or she may be able to handle the fear of loneliness. However when a person he or she has been dating steadily suddenly breaks off the relationship, suicide often occurs. Suicide does not happen for trivial, meaningless reasons, at least not in the eyes of the victim. Suicide is the last straw — the only alternative left — the straw that breaks the camel's back, so to speak. For college students, then, there are some fairly clear characteristics present when suicide might occur.

High school students, on the other hand, paint a different picture. It is a picture very difficult to define even when you see it. A high school student seriously contemplating suicide may be provocative, defiant and rejecting of society as a whole. Yet a great many high school students display this behavior, and they are nowhere near being suicidal.

Some students visibly display self-destructive behavior. They drink too much. They drive too fast. If they're not trying to kill themselves, they're going to kill someone else for sure. Again, these characteristics are present in so many young people. How can we know which ones are suicidal?

The answer is we don't. That's why, as parents or concerned Christian adults, we need to know more about our young people today. Perhaps they are not suicidal at all. However open defiance and self-destructive behavior are signs of some problem, a problem adults need to deal with. The point is adults need to be more concerned with the lives of our young people. What are they doing? What are they saying? How do they think and feel about things? If they are thinking about suicide, an adult somewhere should know about it.

The sad and dangerous part of high school suicides is that sometimes they are impossible to know or find out. Some very caring and communicating parents have lost children to suicide. You see, high school suicides can be outstanding students, high achievers, with tremendous personalities, liked and loved by everyone. High school suicides can come from Christian families. They can be surrounded by loving and caring adults ready and willing to listen and help. The truth is these students feel alone even in a crowd. They feel they have failed even though they get straight "A's" and have been accepted by a fine college.

Suicide deals with feelings. Whether the feelings are real or imagined simply doesn't matter. Feelings cause suicide, and so these feelings are dangerous. They need to be dealt with. It is difficult to deal with the feelings of a person displaying some very defiant behavior. Still for us as Christians their behavior should not make them less deserving of our care and help. Jesus ministered to the undesireables of his time.

The truly difficult part of dealing with a person who is defiant is that he or she may not want our help. Teenagers who display defiant and self-destructive behavior may be more easily perceived as suicidal, still they are the most difficult cases to help and to find help for. These are cases where a caring Christian community can be of great help. It is not only the young person who needs help, but the entire family needs support and guidance.

If a young person in your church or community is exhibiting defiance, is in trouble with the law, perhaps even in jail, communicate through letters or visits if possible. Your show of concern and support can make a difference. Don't stop with the young person, but also give support to the family. Families feel guilt and shame over what a child has done. These feelings tend to drive them from church and the Christian support and fellowship they need. Show your support so they know they are welcome in your church. Let them know they can talk to you and come to you for the support they need. Pray for the whole family always.

Our Christian responsibility is in the support we give. Being a youth counselor in your church can be the means of support. However there are many ways we can reach youth. Support their activities. Offer to drive. Give them financial support. Attend their fund raisers.

The support of the family can come through the message we bring to Bible class and to all the people we talk to. If the family is important to us, others should know it. If caring for others is important to us, others should see our example.

What a tremendous witness Christian families and individuals can be to our world. It is suffering some great losses. This can be seen in the effect on our teenagers. Suicide is evidence of some very deep and overwhelming problems. In dealing with suicide we can also deal with these problems. We can begin to understand the problems and pains felt by suicidal individuals.

Sometimes a suicide note will spell out the inner problems and conflicts felt by the individual. A note is usually left by a person who has thought a lot about him or herself and the problems of life. An analysis of a suicide note can usually give some idea of how the person who wrote it actually felt inside. Compare the number of suicides in our country with the number of notes left, and suicide notes are fairly rare. The majority of suicide victims are not in touch with their feelings. Perhaps they could not say why they chose suicide.

Studies show that feelings, real or imagined, which revolve around the lack of self-worth cause suicides. People with suicidal thoughts generally consider themselves worthless to themselves and to the world. They lack purpose. They feel life isn't worth living. They believe their feelings will never change. They feel hopeless and helpless with no way out, except maybe by committing suicide. Nothing will ever change to make a difference or to make them happy.

Unhappy, rather than happy, is another important term to understand about suicide, especially teenage suicide. Unhappiness is different from depression. Depression is what Freud determined as the cause of suicide. In today's terms it is an emotional illness that can be cured. We all feel unhappy many times. Although no one wants to be unhappy, unhappiness has never been a determined cause of suicide, until now. Yes, teenage suicide has been determined to be caused by unhappiness.

It's important to remember that teenage problems are not always huge, that is compared to adult problems. But teenage problems are indeed traumatic for teenagers. One Minnesota paper recorded: "Braces Cause Teenage Suicide." In many cases very small, almost simple problems have either piled up or been blown up way out of proportion by the adolescent state of mind. Adolescence changes a young person, not only in how he or she looks but even changes feelings. One very strong feeling that comes during adolescence is inadequacy.

On the scale of life adolescence weighs in overweight. Sure there are changes to go through, problems to face. Insecurities overwhelm many teenagers. Today we have to add the lack of family support, loss of religious community and declining moral values. Still we must remember that people live through adolescence no matter how heavily the problems weigh upon them. Perhaps we would do well to begin studies on how they make it through. We would most likely see they found their needed support somewhere along the way. But for those who aren't making it through, for those who haven't or simply can't find the support they need, for those who are contemplating death rather than facing life — for those, this book is written.

Some of the facts about teenage suicide are staggering. The truth is, though, that we've barely touched the surface. So much more needs to be learned to prevent teenage suicide.

First of all, we should know that suicide has been an accepted practice in many countries and cultures. In the Fiji Islands it was a common practice for the wives of chieftains to kill themselves upon the deaths of their husbands. In India suttee, where the widow was burned on her husband's funeral pyre, was practiced well into the 1900s. Some African tribes had a rule that if one person caused another person to kill himself that person must also kill himself. Suicide was practiced among American Indian tribes. If a man lost face, he could regain honor by committing suicide. The Chinese accepted suicide as a way for a defeated ruler or general to regain honor. In Japan samurai warriors committed hara-kiri to obtain honor for themselves. Even today Japan has an extremely high suicide rate. Judaism regards suicide as a sin, but honors suicide committed to avoid being murdered, forced to worship idols or heathen gods, sold into slavery or sexually abused.

The Bible records some suicides or deaths comparable to suicide. In Judges 9:50-55 Abimelech asked his armor-bearer to kill him. Samson in Judges 16:23-31 asked God to let him die with the Philistines. In 1 Samuel 31:1-6, 2 Samuel 1:1-27 and 1 Chronicles 10:1-14 we read that Saul fell on his own sword and killed himself. Ahithopel hanged himself according to 2 Samuel 17:23. That Zimri burned himself to death in the palace is recorded in 1 Kings 16:8-20. As recorded in Matthew 27:3-10 and verified in Acts 1:16-20, Judas hanged himself. The theological implications of suicide will be discussed in the last chapter.

From the first Pentecost down to the present Christian attitudes about suicide have gone through some radical changes. The early Christian church was severely persecuted. Believers were put to death for their faith. They were called martyrs. Stephen was the first martyr according to Acts 7:54-60.

When persecuted Christians no longer wanted to live, they began to see martyrdom as a glorified and certain means of being saved. During the fourth and fifth centuries Christians were caught up in suicide mania. One preacher, John Donne, taught that martyrdom afforded certain redemption. His followers called Donatists possessed a genuine lust for martyrdom. They demanded their own executions.

St. Augustine enunicated the doctrine that suicide allows no opportunity for repentance. He branded suicide a crime and sin against God's plan. It was an act inspired by the devil. Suicide's connection with the devil brought about certain superstitions.

A suicide was buried at the crossroads. The traffic was supposed to keep the evil spirit from rising. A stone over the face or a stake through the heart would do the same thing. The number of roads was supposed to confuse the spirit and make it impossible for the spirit to find its way back home. The Christian symbol of the cross was to dispel the evil energy of the body. All this was done in an effort to protect persons who might feel they had caused the suicide.

A tremendous amount of guilt arises in those close to a suicide victim. From what Christians hold true about suicide today, we can see how dealing with suicide would hold a lot of fear and superstition. We can see how concerned Christians would reject anyone who committed suicide and even those close to a suicide victim. We can begin to see why concerned and caring Christians do not wish to deal with someone who is even thinking about suicide. A Christian could feel any contact with such a person or with such thoughts might place their own faith and salvation in jeopardy.

We forget that sin and superstition and fear have nothing to do with the will of God. We need to be reminded that sin and death have no power over us. We must remember that nothing "will be able to separate us from the love of God that is in Christ Jesus our Lord" (Romans 8:38). Indeed our faith and salvation are secure in the death and resurrection of our Lord Jesus Christ. And we have a Christian responsibility for our fellow human beings.

It's time we allowed our Christian responsibility and love to reach out to teenagers, especially to those who are experiencing the traumas of their adolescence and of an anomic society. When we reach out to teenagers experiencing problems that may even include suicidal thoughts, we don't want to condemn them. We want to try to understand why they are considering death over life. We want to comfort and counsel them so that they see other alternatives to solving their pains and problems.

There's a Bible story that can help us see how we can counsel and help someone thinking about or wanting to die. In 1 Kings 19:1-8 one of God's great prophets, Elijah, asked to die. We'll be using this story about Elijah in greater detail later in this book. It might be good for you to read it and become familiar with it now. Take special note of how God listened to Elijah and of what God did to help Elijah overcome his desire to die.

In Philippians 1:23 the Apostle Paul writes of his desire to be with Christ. This is not a death wish. Paul's life was one of suffering, still he didn't allow his sufferings to overpower him. On the contrary, as we read on in Philippians, we find Paul was filled with joy. Suicides are never filled with joy.

Christians need to follow the examples given to us by God through his holy Word. God does not want suicide. He does not approve of suicide. Killing anyone including yourself is a sin. Still, God through Christ does not condemn sinners, but offers us forgiveness. For those thinking of suicide this very minute God is offering you his forgiveness, his love and his peace. Indeed, God wants everyone to be saved and to come to know him and love him and rest in his arms of peace and joy. Read 1 Timothy 2:4.

We have discovered that teenagers are facing some difficult problems and that they are facing them all alone. Teenagers have been left to grow up all alone. In the remaining chapters of this book we will be discussing why teenagers are growing up all alone, and what Christians can do to help teenagers want to live and know the peace and joy of Christ.

Two
Good Old Days

We often hear people talking about the good old days. They say things like, "We never had a lot of money, but we always had a lot of love." Everyone had a job to do, and everyone worked hard. Still they always took time for each other. They found time to talk and visit.

Those were the days when people had a whole bunch of kids too. Many lived on farms. The more hands they had to help, the better off they were. Children were needed, and they knew they were needed.

Feeding all those extra mouths was not a problem, either, not on the farm where vegetables and meat were available. New clothing was expensive, but then who ever bought new clothing? Everyone would wear patched and repatched hand-me-downs until they were nothing more than rags. Then the rags were used too.

Times must have been hard, but nobody seems to remember that. Maybe those huge family gatherings erased all the bad memories. There were so many people at your house no one could hardly move. Those times you could eat all you wanted, run anywhere you wanted and you felt free. You didn't have a problem in the world.

If there were problems, the whole family worked them out. There was always someone to talk to. There was always someone who listened to you too. Families were a lot closer then. They needed each other.

Whole families attended church together on Sunday, services and Sunday school in the morning. Going to church wasn't always a matter of jumping in a car and arriving at church in ten minutes. Some folks had to walk or ride for hours to get to church. They didn't mind. They felt the worship and fellowship were important and needed by their families.

If a family didn't show up for church, everyone missed them. The minister was usually on his way to find out why the next morning. It wasn't uncommon to have neighbors or friends checking on them, just to make sure they were all right. Most of the time when people missed church, there was a real problem.

Sure they had problems. Didn't everyone? They had sickness. Old Doc would fix that. Nobody seems to even remember a time when Doc couldn't fix someone up. They had death. It just wasn't any great big deal. Everybody was born and lived and died. That was the way it was. People just did the best they could. Those were the good old days!

Then along came progress. Parents wanted things better for their children. Children felt they could have a better, easier life than their parents had. They began to leave the protection of the farm and family. They moved to the city.

It's true the city offered a lot of potential for earning a good living. Farming never paid a real salary to speak of. If you got a job in the city, you worked for wages. On payday you had real money to spend. Never had that on the farm, no siree.

It didn't turn out so well for everyone who gave up farming. Some didn't find jobs in the city that paid enough to support them and their families, if they had families. People still believed in having large families. So, if you had a family to support, it was usually a large one.

Back on the farm children helped with the work. It was kind of natural to put them to work in the city too. During the industrial revolution children worked hard, long hours for very little pay. Some of their employees were cruel and uncaring. In fact people who moved to the city found that the city itself was cold and uncaring.

The city offered financial opportunities. It did not offer the close and caring atmosphere of the farm family. People who lived together in the same city didn't know each other. Once they had their jobs they were too busy. A farmer could take time out from a busy day and stop to visit a neighbor. In the city an employer told you where you had to be, when and even exactly what you had to do.

The problem of child labor eventually worked itself out. The cruel and uncaring treatment of children in the labor force came to the attention of humanitarians. These humanitarians paved the way for children's rights and for their protection by the law.

Children were no longer allowed to work long hours. Now they were sent to school to receive education and training. Trained and educated children would be more valuable to society in the long run. So it seemed the problem of child labor worked itself out nicely, except for one fact, the feelings of the children were never really considered.

When children were liberated from labor, they were assigned to schools. They were expected to perform, to study hard and make something of themselves. Who knows, if they succeed, children might even be valuable again someday?

Society's move from agriculture to industry does not appear to be very pretty when seen through the eyes of the children. It is these changes that started right after the good old days that are tearing our children apart even today. Somewhere through all these changes children lost their value and worth.

Children continue to be on the losing end of the things. Children today are left to grow up all alone. They probably feel they aren't important. Maybe some of them even feel their parents don't love them enough.

Now this is how children are reported to feel. It is not necessarily true. Most parents feel their children are important, and they love their children very much. It is circumstances that have caused children and teenagers to feel unimportant and unloved. Feelings, real or imagined, cause teenage suicide.

Lack of self-esteem and self-worth is a predominant characteristic of teenage suicides. When teenagers lack worth and value, they need help. Where do teenagers today go for help? They used to be able to go to their families.

Families today have been juggled into anything we want them to be. The traditional father, mother and children roles are unrecognizable. Every member of the family is left to do his or her own thing. Anyone who tries to define the male or female role is faced with recrimination. This is the family to which a teenager must go for guidance and answers.

To be able to find out who they are and determine their value teenagers need examples to follow. Teenagers find out who they are by discovering who their parents are. They determine their worth by how valuable their parents consider them to be.

This information is not available to teenagers growing up all alone. Families are no longer close. They are spread out over every job, hobby and activity imaginable. Families are also small. From siblings to grandparents there just aren't very many of them to talk to. The extended family — aunts, uncles and cousins usually live a distance away. The family gatherings no longer exist. Putting the whole family into a farm house is one thing, but try squeezing them all into a condominium and see what happens.

It's obvious a teenager is hard pressed to obtain help from the family, such as it is. An extended family might be of help, but is unavailable. So where does a teenager go for guidance and understanding?

A teenager used to be able to go to church. The minister always seemed to be there when needed, or a Sunday school teacher or youth leader. Even the little old lady who patted all the children on the head and told them how precious they all were was a big help.

Going to church isn't like that anymore. For one thing, people don't go to church. Ministers are as busy as everyone else. There still are Sunday school teachers and youth leaders, even some little old ladies. But Sunday school classes are badly attended. Youth leaders have a hard time getting enough youth to make a meeting worthwhile. And nobody notices little old ladies or cares what they have to say.

Well, what about faith and prayer? Teenagers have their individual faith in God to give them strength. God is always there for them, to listen and help them. God is always available.

It's true God is always available and can help. However many teenagers today have not been taught to go to God for help. They seemingly have everything they need in life or even want. They don't need faith and prayer to get them through each day. Or do they?

Physically teenagers certainly do have or can obtain most of what they need or want. Spiritually they lack a great deal. Many lack purpose and the knowledge of God's plan for their lives.

Teenagers don't know who they are or where they're going. The family was designed to teach them that. God designed the family to be a close, caring and supportive unit. That closeness begins at the moment one man and one woman become one. Read Genesis 2:24; Matthew 19:5; Ephesians 5:31.

"The family that prays together stays together," did not simply pop out of nowhere. God designed the family to live together in him and according to his plan. Faith and prayer keep a family strong and keep them together.

Statistics prove that a lower divorce rate is found among the churched than among the unchurched. A lower divorce rate still is found among families who attend church together on a regular basis. Generally there is a considerable connection between the closeness of the traditional family and their closeness to God. In his Word God gives specific guidelines for the Christian family.

Husbands and wives are to submit to one another. Read Ephesians 5:21. They are to give everything for each other, just as Christ gave everything, even his life, for them.

Children, including teenagers, are commanded to obey and honor their parents. Read Ephesians 6:1-3. God in his wisdom even included a check-and-balance system in Ephesians 6:4. Parents are to afford their children respect and not exasperate their children.

God did not stop with a mere plan. To his plan he gave order, for God is a God of order. Read 1 Corinthians 14:33. He placed the man at the head of the family. God did not do this to cause disharmony or inequality as some would believe. The Bible clearly states that in God's eyes all people are equal. Read Galatians 3:28. The man's headship does not consist of power but of love. Christian love is to be the foundation of the Christian family. Proverbs 31:10-31 gives guidelines for the Christian wife and mother. If followed, God's plan is perfect, for God is perfect. Read Matthew 5:48.

When sin entered the world, it began to slowly chip away at God's perfect plan. The man did not want to be the head of the family with that responsibility. The wife and mother did not feel loved as God had intended. She felt oppressed and used by her husband and children. The children? We already know how teenagers feel — unloved, unwanted and unplaced.

It's true. Teenagers today have been unplaced. They haven't been displaced, that is, banished or ousted. They haven't been misplaced, that is, lost or forgotten. They are unplaced. They seem not to have a place anymore.

They used to have a place. They were members of a family. The family worked together. Every member had a place. All members felt needed and worthwhile. Somehow in the rush of things, in the desire to improve, in the name of progress, they lost their place.

Is this because God has also been lost, or at least set aside? No longer first in our lives? Indeed families are no longer placed first. Husbands are not placing their wives first. Wives are no longer placing their husbands first. Parents no longer place children first. Children no longer place parents first.

We all need to be needed and loved. We all need to be first, to feel important, to feel self-worth. In God through Christ we find our worth. To God we are valuable. We are precious. We are loved. Read John 3:16.

People who are not exposed to God's love through regular Bible study, worship and prayer do not always feel his love. They tend to be more caught up in what they can do than in what God has done for them. Some of these people are teenagers. Some of these teenagers feel so unloved and so unvaluable that they attempt suicide.

There is another part of God's love that we need to explore. Since God loves us so much, we also ought to love one another. Read 1 John 4:11. That makes us want to reach out and help other people.

Suicide has been said to be the most selfish act any person can ever commit. Suicidal thoughts are thoughts totally of self. We need to realize that a happy and fulfilled life doesn't revolve around the self.

It's true that God considers us to be very important. That's why we can feel valuable, because we are loved by him. The Bible says, "Love your neighbor as yourself." Romans 13:9 also implies a self love. First, though, it commands a love for others.

Who or what is first in our lives. Is it the things of the world? Do we place ourselves and what makes us happy first? When we do that we disobey God's command to love others.

We need to place God first in our lives. We need God and his love to know that we are valuable. We need

God and his love to know who we are and where we are going. God has chosen each and every one of us for a very special purpose. Read 1 Peter 2:9,10.

So as God's chosen people we find our purpose. We find the reason for which we were created. It is to share God and his love with others, to bring them to know God through Christ, to have them know his peace.

All identity, all self-worth, all love, all joy and all peace are part of God's plan and purpose for our lives. Yet so many do not see any of these beautiful things God has to offer. Why not? Because society paints a very different picture.

Society teaches living for self. It teaches you must have the most, the best and the newest of everything to be happy. No more patched and repatched hand-me-downs. Society is to provide the best of everything.

Teenagers are very much aware of this. Society or their parents are to provide them with all that they desire. Not only do they not need God, but seemingly they do not need anything. They have everything. They have nothing to wait for, nothing to dream about.

What is left for teenagers to hope for? What is left to be accomplished? How can teenagers plan for the future? What goals can they actually reach?

These are some of the questions teenagers are facing. They are important questions. They are questions adults find hard to answer. Still teenagers are being asked to deal with and answer these questions. And circumstances in our society leave our youth to answer them all alone.

We do well to look at the world through the eyes of some teenagers. We need to realize we have a lot of teenagers. Childhood illnesses have been conquered by modern medicine. More and more children are reaching their teens. If teenagers are to succeed and feel they are valuable members of society — teenagers must compete for their place of success. And the competition is fierce!

Just what will they accomplish? What is left? Perhaps a cure for cancer or the common cold. Either one would be great, but the individual's chances of accomplishing either one are pretty slim at best.

To be able to explore new territories one would have to join the space program. Talk about strong competition. How many astronauts are there in our country today? How many get chosen to fly a space mission?

What does the world have to offer teenagers? Well, there's pollution, and loss of natural resources. Crime is running rampant; prisons are overcrowded. And we could be in the midst of a nuclear war at any moment.

Through the eyes of elderly persons things look pretty grim, but a good share of their life has been lived already. A middle-aged person finds the whole situation very distressing and hopes the world will hang on till he or she no longer has need of it. The teenager wonders, "Why should I try to go on living in a world that's just going to blow itself up anyway?"

The entire situation looks pretty devastating through the eyes of teenagers today. It doesn't have to be that way. Teenagers don't have to feel they have nothing left to hope for, to accomplish. They have a future because God in his grace and love and mercy planned for a future.

When the time was right, God sent his Son . . . to redeem us . . . to make us his children . . . to give us eternal life. Read Galatians 4:4-7. This was and is God's plan from the beginning for all believers, for all teenagers who know and believe in Christ.

The problem is that teenagers who know Christ and believe in him are not that familiar with God's plan. They have not had the education or the opportunity to develop in a personal relationship with Jesus Christ. They tend to believe that their identity and self-worth comes from something they must accomplish, rather than through what Christ has already accomplished for them.

Christ offers hope for the future. He offers a plan and gives each individual a purpose, sharing his love and forgiveness. In the end he offers eternal life. There is nothing temporary about Christ. Teenagers needn't worry that all he offers will ever change. Read Hebrews 13:8. Nowhere else will teenagers find the certainty and stability they so desperately need, except in Christ.

A personal relationship with Christ begins in the family. Christian parents bring their children to Christ in baptism. Children learn to know Christ through their parents. Regular church attendance strengthens the relationship. Family devotions, Bible study and prayer help the relationship to grow. It all begins in the home with the family, just like in the good old days.

However we know that the family today has taken some dangerous beatings. It has suffered massive breakdown. Where does a teenager go to learn more about Christ? Even Christian families suffer from lack of time to give support in a very busy world. Where do concerned Christian parents turn for help to have their children learn to know Jesus as Savior, Shepherd, Friend?

Christian education through the church's educational agencies is the answer. Certainly regular Sunday school attendance will be of help in closing up gaps parents may not be able to fill. A Christian day school can also be of immense help and support to parents.

Some parents do not believe Christian day schools are necessary. Their children can be educated in public schools just as well. There are some parents who feel their children will receive a better education in a public school. To debate this issue parents need to ask themselves, "What is a good education? Do we want our children to know about things of the world or about Christ?" In a Christian day school children learn both. They also learn to place the wisdom of the world into proper perspective and to see what knowledge is most important to their salvation.

Some children attend Christian day schools for eight years. Then their parents feel they should attend public high schools to spread their wings, to see what it's like in the real world.

But teenagers spread their wings in Christian high schools too. They become aware of the real world. The difference is they find out about life in a caring and Christian atmosphere. They are taught to use their Christian education to help them make their decisions in a secular and humanistic world. The same holds true for Christian colleges and universities. Christian education stresses the one thing necessary to properly define our love for ourselves and for others, God's great love for us through his Son Jesus Christ.

Still it's true the family may fail to give teenagers Christian training. It's even true that Christian education may not pave a complete path to Christ. So it then becomes the job of adult Christians to step out and show teenagers the way.

Adult Christians could make themselves available to teenagers. They could become youth leaders or Bible class teachers. They could attend or financially support youth activities. They could share a smile or simply present a warm and caring attitude. They could place teenagers they know and those they don't know on their prayer lists.

Concerned adult Christians have tremendous potential for bringing teenagers into a better relationship with Christ. Christ is the answer to all the troubles teenagers are experiencing today. This is not to say Christ will take away all troubles. This is not to say Christ will completely do away with teenage suicide. A personal relationship with Christ does not automatically free us of all our troubles. We do, however, receive the strength to deal with our troubles.

The Apostle Paul's life seemed overcome with problems and pain. To begin with Paul, or Saul — his name at first, was directly responsible for the persecution of many Christians. He held the coats of and agreed with the men who stoned Stephen to death.

Imagine the guilt of all those persecutions and even death Paul must have felt. Through God's forgiveness and strength Paul dealt with his guilt. He went on to become perhaps the greatest apostle.

Paul also suffered from some type of physical malady. It must have been painful, sometimes unbearable. He asked God to take it away. God's answer recorded in 2 Corinthians 12:9 is, "My grace is sufficient for you, for my power is made perfect in weakness."

God was saying more than No to Paul. God was saying your pain and your troubles allow you to be strong. Likewise our troubles give us the opportunity to go to God for help through our prayers. As we come to know God more and more and to trust in him, we become strong enough to handle the troubles that come our way.

Paul also suffered persecution for being a Christian. Paul did not see it as suffering though. He considered his suffering unimportant compared to the glories that would one day be his in heaven.

The Apostle Paul's life has a lot to say to teenagers or anyone who is thinking of using suicide to solve their problems. Problems do not give us the right to commit suicide. Problems show us how much we desperately need God.

God helped Paul handle his problems and pains. Paul wrote many letters while he was in prison. He was no doubt uncomfortable and probably in pain. Yet his letters are full of joy. He rejoiced in his suffering. He rejoiced in his hope. He rejoiced in his salvation through his Lord and Savior Jesus Christ.

What a tremendous example Paul is for us when the troubles of life get us down. Paul's story can be very helpful when dealing with a teenager thinking of suicide. Problems that seem overwhelming become a means of drawing closer to God, to his love, to his comfort, to his power. This allows us to deal with our troubles, even rejoice in them.

Paul could be writing directly to teenagers today when he wrote Romans chapter eight. In verses 1 through 13, Paul assures all believers that they are free from condemnation. They are free from all guilt because they are forgiven through Jesus Christ.

Paul knows the world would have us believe otherwise. Our sinful self tells us we must look good or successful in the eyes of the world. In verse 6 Paul writes, "The mind of sinful man is death, but the mind controlled by the Spirit is life and peace." The Holy Spirit motivates us to live not for self but for God and for others. That's success in God's eyes.

In verses 14 through 17 Paul is telling teenagers they can boldly stand and face their problems. Why? Because they are the children of God. They can be certain. They can be confident. They can be joyful. They are heirs with Christ to the blessings of heaven itself.

Paul doesn't stop when he tells them they can face their problems. In verses 18 through 25 he explains why and how their problems should be viewed or handled. Paul says they can do it because there are better days ahead. He takes us right inside the mind of the possible teenage suicide who feels things will never change, never be any better. Paul says, "You are wrong! Things are going to be better. Gloriously better."

We may have to give up certain things on earth, things like worldly treasures or pleasures. These are small things and worthless compared to what awaits us in heaven.

In verses 26 and 27 Paul warns teenagers. Don't try to make it alone. Everyone needs somebody. Circumstances in society leave teenagers growing up all alone. Paul says, "It doesn't have to be that way." God is always available.

Teenagers today need to know they are never alone, not when they have God to turn to. Parents, families and friends may be too busy. They may be far away. God is never too busy. He is always just a prayer away.

God knows teenagers too. He isn't someone who doesn't understand adolescence and growing up. God created growing up. He created every detail and every stage and every feeling. He understands, and he feels. He can and will help those who love him. Read verses 28-30.

Sometimes teenagers, especially those contemplating suicide, feel so unlovable. They feel they don't deserve to be loved by God or by anyone else. It doesn't matter how we feel about ourselves. God loves us anyway. He called us to be members of his family, his sons and daughters, through baptism and the gospel. We share with Christ in eternal salvation. And nothing, absolutely nothing, can separate us from God and his love for us.

32   There isn't a person alive who doesn't need to be loved. What a wonderful gift Christians have to share when we share God's love! It is a love that is certain and lasting. It will never fade away. Each time we share it we find it has grown within us. The more we give it away, the more it is returned to us.

All that loving kind of takes us back to the good old days, the time when families were close to God and to each other. Then people took time to care what happened to other people. Then children and teenagers felt needed and loved.

Doesn't that describe the Christian family God wants us to be? The good old days were when people who loved God shared their love for God with each other. We still have people like that. People who are reading this book and asking themselves, "What can I do to help? What can I do to make a difference?" With a lot of Christian care and concern, by awakening ourselves and society to the needs of teenagers today, we can make a difference.

Who knows if years from now our teenagers will be referring to their times of trouble and pain as the good old days simply because we took time to care? For then they will have more fully realized how their troubles and pains brought them to a closer personal relationship with their Lord and Savior, Jesus Christ.

Three
Identity Crisis

"My grandfather was a doctor. My father was a doctor. I am a doctor. So that settles it. You're going to be a doctor too."

Most parents aren't quite so emphatic about their children's choice of occupation. They are proud to have a son or daughter follow in their footsteps. If their children choose another career, it's all right too. Of course there are parents who get upset or even angry with their child's choice. There are also some children who feel threatened because they feel they must be whatever their parents want them to be.

There are countries in the world where children are expected to follow in their parents' footsteps. In India the caste system seldom allows for a man to be anything but what his father was. Americans in general would find this practice totally unfair. Children, they feel, should have the right to make their own decisions about what they want to do in life.

Studies show that young people who do not have to choose their occupation are under less pressure than those who do. These studies do not hold true in America where the freedom of choice predominates. However they could prove that pressures are a result of society not of adolescence. That's not to say children should become carbon copies of their parents to solve the problems of the world. It merely shows that adolescent problems need to be dealt with in the context of our society.

Our society has encouraged parents to give their children space. Children have been allowed to do their own thing. Each individual is supposed to find out what's best for him or her. Society in general is saying, "Leave your children alone."

Children should be allowed to discover certain areas of life on their own. They have to decide what makes them happy or unhappy. They need space all their own to learn, to grow and to discover their identity. However parents and educators are finding the space has gotten too large. Teenagers no longer feel on their own; they feel all alone.

Teenagers are feeling a huge void in their lives. Something is missing, and they don't know what it is. It's been described as growing up in a vacuum. It becomes so overwhelming that teenagers are turning to drugs and alcohol just to fill it up. All the space they have fills them with fear. They've become afraid to discover their identity.

In our effort to free our children we have placed them in a horrid prison. We have forced them to set up protective boundaries that neither parents nor teenagers can break down. These boundaries actually keep teenagers from making decisions. At the same time they force teenagers to remain teenagers for a very long time. Or should we say adolescence lasts through college and even beyond?

It happens because parents are willing and able to support their children for as long as necessary. They provide them with all their physical needs. They support them financially through college and even into their married life.

A problem teenagers face, besides lack of family, religion and moral support, is too much of everything else. Everything they have has to be new too. One of the complaints voiced most often by parents is that their teens expect everything to be new. Parents complain their budget can't possibly handle a teenager, to say nothing of two or three. Then there are the parents who can't afford to buy things new, but buy them anyway. This creates problems with the budget. It also creates resentment from siblings who can't have what the teenager in the family is getting.

Parents, who say No, stand to face some strong defiance from an angry teenager. Teenagers who go without the new face some pretty devastating peer pressure. It is truly a no-win situation. Unless, of course, the teenager can rely upon the Christian principles taught in the Bible that show us things are not important. And parents who realize that things are not importnat will no longer feel guilty about not providing them.

Parents also need to realize that things can become substitutes for giving of their time. Parents may feel that, if they shower their teenagers with things they want, they make up for not giving them things they need, like parental love and support and by simply being available to listen and talk to them.

A recent study shows that American parents spend an average of fourteen minutes communicating with their teenagers during a given week. We may be shocked at that small amount of time. We may even think the study must be wrong. The key word here, remember, is communicating. We may be with our teenagers. We may be taking them here, there and everywhere. But that is not communicating. Communicating is time spent together where you learn something about your teenager. At the same time your teenager is learning something about you. It is a time of open and honest conversation and of learning.

It is important for parents and teenagers to spend time communicating. During the adolescent years teenagers are constantly developing their values. Teenagers need adults to be able to develop their values. Adolescents look at the values of their parents and other adults. They weigh what they find out against what they already feel and know. Problems arise when adolescents cannot or do not communicate with adults who possess strong values. When they have nothing to weigh their thoughts against they come up with zero.

We can add to this the problems faced by parents with strong values. It seems parents who are concerned, who are communicating and who want teenagers to have good examples and Christian values are becoming confused. In this confusion parents are facing mid-life crises, divorces and other serious problems of their own. They want to help. They are concerned. They just can't seem to solve their own problems much less the problems of their teenagers.

Some of these problems stem from a lack of strong Christian principles and teachings in our society. However these problems are happening also among

Christians and within Christian families as well as outside Christianity. We need to realize that teenage problems and especially teenage suicide happen to people and families regardless of race or religion. As Christians we have so very much to offer teenagers in terms of what God has given us. We ought not feel that helping teenagers is beneath Christianity or beneath us. We are helping human beings just like us. We are all sinners. Read Romans 3:23.

Some of the teenagers who need our help the most have truly gone in a very wrong direction. We need to remember they have strayed because they did not have any one to help them in the right direction. Adolescents need adults, and one way or another they will find adult support. The adults they find may not give them the right support.

An adult who deals in drugs will look for adolescents who are desperate for adult love and attention. This adult will pretend to care for the adolescents, but at the same time he or she will be getting the adolescents hooked on drugs. The next step is turning the adolescent into a drug dealer. The adolescent may or may not catch on to the scheme. Once hooked on drugs it's too late to escape. Adolescent dealers need the drugs, the supplier and the money to support their habit.

Leaders of various religious cults look for adolescents who feel unloved. The drawing card of every cult is that a person will find the loving community he or she is searching for. Once committed the cult uses mind control to keep you there. Improper nourishment, overwork and taking all of your worldly possessions make you totally dependent on the cult for survival.

Over one million teenagers run away from home every year. They've had a disagreement or some sort of break in the family relationship. Some of them have been physically or sexually abused. Others have been asked to leave because their family could no longer support them. The reason doesn't really matter. The effect is these adolescents feel unloved. They have been rejected by adults and turned out to find their way in the world, alone and uncared for. Many adolescent runaways get caught up in the horrors of child pornography and prostitution. They are caring for and supporting themselves because no one else will.

We can easily see why an adolescent caught up in drugs, in a cult or in pornography and prostitution might see suicide as a way out. It's true we may find these adolescents heavily involved in crime. They place little value on their lives or any human life. These adolescents may lie, steal, rob or even murder. However these adolescents do not make up a very large percentage of teenage suicides. Why not? Because these adolescents are survivors. They are determined to live against all odds and at any cost. Their circumstances would be shocking for most people, but these adolescents have learned to survive.

Teenage suicides have lost or simply given up the desire to survive. That is what's so shocking. Suicide more often than not occurs among adolescents who have everything to live for. Of course allowing our adolescents to become involved in drugs, cults and prostitution is not an answer to the teenage suicide problem. We want adolescents to grow into productive and successful adults. And the solution comes with our taking the time to help them grow.

Teenagers today are given too little support and too much of everything else. Parents are busy and unable to find time to be with their children. When children become teenagers, they are expected to be on their own. Why not let them go? Teenagers are almost grown up. They are not grown up all the way. How often we hear, "Those kids know so much more than I did at their age." Do they really know so much more? Or do we expect them to know so much more? Adolescents receive a better education than past generations received. But education does not pass anyone through adolescence any faster. Adolescence is the time for a young person to learn and grow.

We may condemn adults who force children to run away and live in the streets before they are ready. What are we doing when we force adolescents to become adults before they are ready? Teenagers are not adults capable of carrying out adult responsibilities. Neither are they children willing to listen to and obey every parental directive and desire. Teenagers are adolescents.

Teenagers need the years of adolescence to establish their identity, to sit back and observe and to find out certain things about themselves and others. They need time to grow into adults. In our society teenagers have been given many of the responsibilities but few of the privileges of adulthood. We have given teenagers more to handle but less training and support to handle life with. We have made teenagers more vulnerable to stress and exposed them to more powerful stresses than any other generation ever faced. Is it any wonder some of them turn to suicide rather than face life?

Some adolescents do not choose suicide but turn to other types of self-destruction, such as drug and alcohol abuse. The National Institute on Alcohol Abuse and Alcoholism reports conservatively that 1.3 million juveniles between the ages of twelve and seventeen have serious drinking problems. One junior high school survey shows 65 percent of the thirteen-year-olds had used alcohol that year. The report states that these young persons received the alcohol from their parents, who were relieved their children weren't using drugs.

Not only have alcohol and drugs become more accessible, also they have become more needed. Teenagers are beginning to feel they cannot face life without them.

Studies have shown that many teenagers attempting suicide use drugs and alcohol regularly. Research has also shown that once the teenager is taken off drugs and alcohol the suicidal tendencies diminish. In many cases the tendencies and thoughts have disappeared entirely.

Another reported type of self-destructive behavior that could lead to teenage suicide is premature sex. People who have had early sexual relations report that it virtually destroyed healthy sexual relations later on. Sexual activity is used to relieve the tension teenagers feel. It can also be used to alleviate the loneliness they suffer. Today by the age of nineteen at least seventy percent of young women have had at least one sexual experience. For young men the percentage is even higher.

Our Lord created sex to be a beautiful expression of love within the bonds of marriage. Outside of marriage the sexual act makes one feel full of guilt and shame. These feelings lead to loss of self-worth and self-esteem. Loss of self-worth and self-esteem lead to teenage suicide.

Violence is another form of self-destructive behavior. Violence to self and violence to others leads to feelings of destruction and many times to suicide. Violence has become an accepted condition of life in America. The average child will have seen 17,000 violent acts on TV by the time he or she enters college. Suicide is a violent act. Analysis has shown suicidal people have repressed murderous impulses. Suicide becomes an escape from killing someone else.

All these forms of self-destructive behavior can and do lead to teenage suicide. Parents and adults in general are not aware of how they work. Teenagers commit suicide so unexpectedly because the cause of suicide is often unexpected.

The parent who provides alcohol for thirteen-year-olds really believes he or she is warding off drug abuse. Do parents realize they may be setting their child up to be another teenage suicide statistic?

Our society provides birth control for teenagers because it is thought better than teenage pregnancy, unwanted children or abortion. Does society realize it is placing a teenager into premature sex which could cause her to take her own life?

We allow our children to watch one violent TV program right after another. Can we possibly know we are contributing to any portion of violent feelings that would one day cause them to kill themselves?

We can be thankful to God that he does not allow adults to fully realize every bit of damage we cause to our children. Indeed we are not perfect, and we make many mistakes. God forgives our mistakes and helps us out more times and in more ways than we can imagine.

Still we need to be aware of some of the damage our actions could cause to children and teenagers. We all need to be aware of the damage child abuse can cause. Some parents may feel child abuse is causing physical injury to a child. Physical injury is abuse, but it is not the only type of abuse. Abuse can be neglect, unjust discipline, derogatory name calling, threatening or direct physical abuse and sexual abuse.

Child abuse of any type is demeaning. It causes children to lose their self-esteem. Children who are abused feel they must be very bad to deserve such treatment. Teenage suicides often occur when teens feel that they no longer deserve to live.

There certainly are many areas where concerned Christians can intervene on behalf of adolescents. There is a great need to establish strong Christian principles and goals in American families. We can see the need for adolescents to have families or supportive adults available to them.

Families need to sit down together and redefine their roles and values. Children need to grow up knowing who they are. They are children of God. They are a part of God's divine plan and purpose. They are valuable and important and loved. They are saved. Their identity is in Christ.

Teenagers who have grown up knowing who they are and how valuable they are will not suffer the severe inadequacies which lead to teenage suicide. They will not need to look any further than God's Word to find their identity and purpose in life.

Families who practice the biblical principle of love for God and one another will find ways to reconcile their differences that presently cause families to break up and break down. They will not be looking to satisfy the self but to serve God and to help each other.

The Bible calls this love *agape* in Greek. It is the love exhibited by God in our Savior Jesus Christ. God did not think of himself when he gave the world his only dear Son. God showed *agape*, love. This love was displayed again by Jesus when he died on the cross for all people. Jesus went through suffering and pain to forgive the sins of others. Indeed Jesus had this love. Read John 15:13.

First Corinthians 13 is often called the love chapter of the Bible. Verses 4 through 7 accurately describe selfless love or *agape*. Love is patient and kind. It is not proud or boastful, self-seeking or rude. Love always protects trusts, hopes and perseveres. Love controls the Christian's life. Anyone who desires to live for Christ lives in love. Read 2 Corinthians 5:14-15. Love binds everything and everyone together in perfect harmony. Read Colossians 3:14.

How does love work? Christians know Christ laid down his life for them. That makes Christians want to give up their lives for others. The greatest gift we can give to God and to others is ourselves. Read 1 John 3:16. Imagine a family living in *agape* love. Parents place God and their children before themselves and their needs. Children turn to God for help and place their parents in the highest realm of respect and love.

Such love is not only selfless, but it is also unconditional. God sent Christ to die for us even though we were miserable sinners. God loved us even when we failed him. He commits himself to us. He chooses to love us no matter what. Read Romans 5:6-8.

How often we hear of families breaking up or breaking down for seemingly legitimate reasons. Some member has done something that in society's eyes is totally unforgivable. It is wonderful to know that God does not look at all our sins and deem them unforgivable.

Picture a family living God's unconditional love. Such a family is willing to forgive the unforgivable, over and over again. Think of a teenager living in the grips of suicidal thoughts and tendencies; then picture a teenager living in the arms of God's unconditional love. What a contribution God's selfless, unconditional love can make to our society today, to the family and to each individual person. Love can be a solution to the problems of our times, especially the problem of teenage suicide.

Love is the answer, but it is not an easy answer. Love doesn't just happen because we want it to. God puts us through some very difficult and usually hard to understand changes. He makes us put our lives in order. He disciplines us to change our ways and to love as he loves us. Read Hebrews 12:6.

For example, God could give us everything we want. Still he doesn't. Why? Because he loves us too much to give us something that would not be good for us. We cannot understand God's wisdom in his choices for us. We do know that when he says No to us it is for our own good. It is because of his great love for us.

As parents we can follow God's example. We can give our children many of the things they ask for. We are financially able to provide for them. We live in a free country where many things are available to us. But we need not feel guilty or afraid to say No to our children. We can plainly see how giving our children all their wishes and desires proves detrimental. Perhaps they cannot see or understand how bad it would be for them to have everything they want, but we can. We say No because we love them so very, very much.

In this same line one more thing needs to be discussed. We often cannot say No to our children because we haven't said No to ourselves. We continue to buy things for ourselves to fulfill our desires. How then can we tell our children they cannot have what we have?

The message is that we adults also need to curb our own desires. It's a different ball game when we begin to live as Christ would have us live. We no longer have such a desire of things. We desire God. We need God's word. We need church, Bible study, family devotions. We need God, and we very much need each other.

Teenagers presently thinking about suicide and especially those attempting it are sending the world a very important message. It is a message we all need to listen to. They are saying that physical needs are not everything.

Teenagers are feeling the lack of some very important emotional and spiritual needs. Materialism and humanism do not satisfy the spiritual needs that are a central part of every human being, that give human beings their identity and their feeling of self-worth.

Teenagers today do not know who they are because they have such a vague idea of what or who their parents want them to be. They don't know where they are going because they've lost adult guidance and direction. To make matters even worse they've been thrown headlong into a society that is no better off then they are. Sometimes they escape. Sometimes they commit suicide.

Adolescents do not sit down and plan ways they can cause problems and disturb society. We have not given them the time to sit down and think about anything. We have given them the world and said, "Take it. It's yours. Now don't bother us anymore."

We have completely done away with the gentle stage of adolescence that everyone needs to go through to get to adulthood. We have forgotten that we were once adolescents. We don't remember the changes we went through, the feelings we had, the mistakes we made, the help and support we had or found for ourselves.

We need to remember that teenagers only appear uncommunicative to the outsider, but their actions, how they dress, the music they listen to communicate so much about them, if we take the time to listen. Teenagers seem to care about little else than how their hair is combed. We need to remember when we cared about how our hair was combed — how we would make it through high school — what we were going to do with the rest of our lives and all those things we never talked about, but surely cared about.

It's time we sat down with our teenagers and became totally honest with them. We could tell them about our own adolescence — how we were afraid of not meeting our parents' expectations or living up to their standards. We could share with them the times we were afraid of being rejected, the times we felt like everyone was making fun of us, the times when we actually failed.

Teenagers need to know that adults are human beings with human frailties. Adults have been through adolescence. They have felt inadequate and useless. They survived those feelings. They learned how to handle their feelings. Adolescents today are not all that different from adolescents of days gone by. Their problems are not so much greater because they're so different. Adolescents' problems seem so much greater because they haven't been taught to handle their problems and emotions.

Problems can tear a person apart, bit by bit, piece by piece. Or problems can teach a person to be stronger, sort of toughen 'em up. The hardest part is understanding or trying to determine why some people fall apart and some people get stronger when confronted with the problems of life. A person who cannot seem to handle little problems is a tower of strength in a crisis. What makes a person able to handle problems? What makes a person unable? The answer is probably as deep as the problems which cause us to ask the question.

It is very much the same with teenage problems, even suicide. Two teenagers in the same environment can suffer virtually the same traumas. One will commit suicide. One will not. That's what makes teenage suicide so untouchable in terms of what exactly causes it. No one can point a finger at just what circumstances must be present before a teenager will take his or her own life.

We know that teenagers need to feel needed and loved. Yet there are so many teenagers in the world who do not feel needed or loved, and they do not even think about suicide. We know teenagers who face rejection or failure can suddenly attempt suicide. Still teenagers are rejected and fail every minute of the day. How many of them actually attempt suicide? Fortunately more teenagers do not attempt suicide than do. We can be thankful there are adolescents who even through tough and troublesome times make their own way.

The world and society in general have handed the teenage population some pretty low blows. We have expected a lot of our teenagers and given very little in return. Still teenagers are living on and trying to cope. They are having dreams and visions of a future that is not always dark and dreary. They have been able to use what they have to make a better life.

Adults need to take notice of the survivors, who are succeeding against the odds we know are present. Find out how they are making it when so many of their fellow teenagers are falling into the grip of teenage suicide. There's a lot of study that needs to be done to determine why some people are suicidal and some are not. Somewhere, somehow the people who make it find the support they need. Maybe they don't require a lot of support.

God made each and every one of us different. We all look differently. We all act differently. Most of us dress and eat differently. It stands to reason that our feelings and needs will be different too. If there is an answer, maybe that is it. We are all individuals. Some of us will be able to handle our problems. Others will allow our problems to handle us. This is a very important point to be aware of in dealing with teenage suicide, especially from the Christian point of view.

Christians tend to feel suicide is not a Christian problem. Christians would never think about suicide, much less attempt it. If they did, they wouldn't be Christians. We need to be fully aware that each Christian is different. After all that is how God made us. Each Christian's faith is different. A Christian may have more faith at one time and less faith at another time in his or her life.

There are so many variables to consider. We can never look at another person who seems to be strong emotionally and say, "Well, that person would never think of suicide." More often than not we would be wrong. Christian teenagers today are seriously considering taking their own lives. We can say that they will never go through with it, that their faith will not allow them to commit suicide. Then we can pick up the newspaper and see that we are wrong.

This is a Christian book on the prevention of teenage suicide. It has been written to help Christians deal with a problem, no, an epidemic present in America right now. Christians need to be aware of it. Christians can help prevent teenage suicides.

If Christians felt that teenage suicide is only a problem outside of Christianity, this book would not need to be written. There are plenty of books on suicide that can be of help to the general population of America. Books on teenage suicide tell that teenagers have lost family, religion and values. They do not explain how to get them back. Those who study suicide realize it stems from feelings of worthlessness and low self-esteem. They do not tell teenagers and their parents how to obtain feelings of worth and value. The Christian can assure them of their value in and through Christ, of their identity as God's Children.

In short, a Christian book is needed because the answers for teenagers thinking of suicide cannot be found anywhere but in Christianity. This book is for Christians and also about Christians. Christians can help in the prevention of teenage suicide. Christians can help each other on a day-to-day basis in all areas of life. Through our understanding teenagers, they can be brought to a better understanding of themselves.

It will take a great deal of time, patience and understanding to make this happen. Above all it will take a great deal of God and his love to make the world a place where teenagers find their true identity in Christ, where there is peace and joy and hope and happiness, even during adolescence.

Four
Adolescence and Adolescents

Adolescence is one of the more difficult parts of life's journey. It is a time when no one seems to understand teenagers. Sometimes they hardly understand themselves. During adolescence life takes a complete turn around, and it's not always for the better either. Young people reach the age of adolescence at different times. A point of reference would be a teenager is an adolescent.

There is one sign of adolescence parents notice almost immediately. One day parents find in the eyes of their adolescent son or daughter they have become totally ignorant. Their ideas are suddenly old fashioned, out of date or just plain stupid. Of course parents don't really turn ignorant over night. It just looks as if they did to teenage son or daughter. Adolescents feel some changes they can't explain. They don't realize they are changing, so they think it must be everyone else who is changing.

The adolescents' world is still pretty narrow. It consists of adults and peers. They can easily see their peers haven't changed. Many of their peers feel the same way they do. So, what's left? Everyone else must mean all those adults. It's a general rule of adolescence not to trust anyone over thirty.

Adolescents' distrust of adults is fairly common. For the most part it's nothing to get really excited about either, unless you are dealing with specific self-destructive behavior.

The combination of self-destructive behavior and mistrust of adults is not only dangerous, but it is also deadly. Why? Teenagers are under the impression that they are indestructible. If anyone over the age of thirty tries to tell them differently, they simply do not believe them.

Some teenagers feel they can drink all the beer they want. They can do drugs. They believe they will never get drunk or hooked on drugs. Others believe they can drive fast and never hurt themselves or anyone else. Then there are the ones who believe they can attempt suicide but never really die.

The facts are that people who drink too much, get drunk; those who take drugs, become addicted; when people drive fast, they kill themselves and other innocent people. Teenagers are not exempt. More and more teenagers are becoming fatal statistics of these facts.

Not believing adults when they state known and proven facts is a symptom of adolescence. So is a feeling called rebellion, not an absolutely bad feeling in itself. Rebellion can be viewed as a healthy way for adolescents to separate from adults and become independent. Adults desire young people to become independent. However adolescents need a certain amount of time to learn to be independent. Independence cannot simply happen over night.

Teenagers often do not realize that they need adult guidance. Without adults around teenagers have no examples on which to base their own identity. Teenagers become mixed up and uncertain about their own lives and values. Teenagers don't understand how much they need adults because adolescence blocks their view. They feel very strongly about their views too. They face some very damaging and grave contradictions in their lives because of their views.

Teenagers will emphatically state that they don't want adult interference in their lives. They may even back this up with some powerfully convincing statements. Yet deep inside they are terribly hurt each time an adult does not interfere or take time to listen and to give advice. Teenagers will try to break off their relationships with parents, even when the relationship has been a very close and caring one. At the very same time they will be dealing with their fear about losing parental love and understanding.

Some adolescents are able to overcome feelings of mistrust and rebellion toward adults. These teenagers live through adolescence with relatively few side effects. Other adolescents are overcome by these same feelings. They suffer through adolescence. Some of them make it through too. Then there are the ones who do not make it. They get caught up in defiant and even criminal behavior. Some of them try self-destructive behavior or even suicide.

Adolescents learn to overcome their feelings of distrust and rebellion through their association with adults who care and display strong values and who have earned the respect of teenagers. With respect comes trust and acceptance. A teenager who has never had the opportunity to get to know an adult will probably not have a high respect for adults. Teenagers who know only adults who have some insecurities and self-doubts about themselves will not find respect for adults. Teenagers will not learn to trust adults when the adults they know display very low and questionable values.

The teenagers' expectations of the world and the people in it are very high. When people prove to be human, with human frailties and inadequacies, teenagers are appalled. Teenagers mistrust and rebel against a world which does not measure up to their standards.

Such are the feelings teenagers and adults deal with during adolescence. The comforting part of all of this is that adolescence does pass and so do feelings of mistrust and rebellion. It is very important for young people approaching the age of adolescence to be forewarned about these common and natural feelings. They need to know that a time may come when they will look at and feel differently about their parents or adults in general. This time and those feelings will pass.

Teenagers should be assured that, even though their feelings may be hard to understand or deal with, they will not be alone. Teenagers should know there are adults who care and will help them through the hard times and difficult feelings.

Adolescence is a time of learning about self for teenagers. It is a time of growing and finding out more about who you are and where you are going. Consequently, as teenagers begin to know themselves better, they begin to understand adults better too. Adolescents often feel that parents are trying to hold them back, not allow them to grow up. As adolescents do grow up, they begin to realize their parents did not want to block their way as much as they wanted to help them on their way.

A story has often been told of the college student who thought her parents were completely outdated before she left for college. During her first year she learned independence was a lot of hard work. It meant growing up and being responsible for yourself. It meant getting to know and understand yourself. One day she wrote a letter to her father that read something like this, "Dad, it's amazing how much you've learned since I've been going to college."

Adolescence then truly can be a state of mind, but there's no denying its reality. Adolescence brings on very real physical as well as emotional changes. Still we need to view these changes as normal and necessary for complete growth and identity for teenagers. We need to take adolescent feelings and problems seriously but not let ourselves be overwhelmed by them. If adults feel adolescence is too great a problem to handle, what are we saying to teenagers who must deal with adolescence?

This is especially true when dealing with teenagers who display suicidal tendencies. These teenagers have somehow gotten the picture that their adolescent problems are too great to handle. They distrust and rebel against the adults who could help them.

These teenagers are in a very difficult and dangerous state. Adults can never really understand this state, even adults who went through adolescence, but never felt suicidal cannot understand. Teenage suicide has been described as indescribable. It cannot be understood by anyone who has not been there personally.

In general suicide has been diagnosed as caused by depression. Clinical depression is described as a state in which no beauty, no love, no hope and no joy exist. There is only a terrible fear and an awful desire to die. It's a living hell. But can we understand how someone

living in hell may prefer to die?

Teenage suicide can be caused by seemingly simple unhappiness. That is why it is so hard to understand. Teenagers become unhappy many times a day. When does their unhappiness become dangerous? When does their unhappiness cause them to become suicidal? The answer is that it is very difficult if not impossible to know. We can, by learning more about teenagers and suicide, know which teenagers may be more susceptible to suicide and be able to help them.

For instance, how do adolescents view suicide? Is it different from how an adult views suicide? Not entirely. Adolescents see suicide not as death, but as an extension of the deadness they already feel deep inside. Adults feel suicide will end their suffering because it ends their life.

Both adults and teens believe suicide will make a change in their painful lives, that suicide offers a peace. Teenagers, however, picture death as a long, peaceful sleep. Adults see it as an end of suffering.

Teenagers and adults attempt suicide for some of the same reasons too. A suicide attempt is a cry for help. Few want to die. They want to be helped.

A teenager who feels like no one notices him or her will attempt suicide to see if someone notices them. Some feel people will suddenly love them when they see how desperate they are. Someone will have to feel sorry for them. These are very immature feelings and only prove their lack of knowledge about suicide.

People who attempt suicide for attention or to somehow receive love do not know or realize that suicide is fatal. They will not be around to actually benefit from their own suicide. If they are successful, they will be dead. It is the same for someone who desires to punish another person by attempting suicide. They cannot gain anything if they are dead.

Lonely or unhappy adolescents picture suicide as a kind of romantic fantasy. They see death as a lover coming to take them away from a world of suffering and pain. Suicide is not a fantasy. It is very real and very deadly. Suicide can also be romanticized by young lovers. They will make a pact to commit suicide together. This is an effort, a false effort, to immortalize their love. In reality they are separating from each other forever. There are also some who feel suicide will reunite them with lost loved ones. This comes from a misunderstanding of biblical information that all Christians will be together with God in heaven.

The biblical teaching that says, "You shall not murder," destroys the hope of such a reunion. It's true no one can say without question that anyone who dies by suicide will not be saved. Salvation is a matter of being forgiven. No one can say whether a suicide victim had the opportunity to repent and be forgiven. But no one can know for sure that a suicide victim will be saved either.

As Christians our hope is in the Lord. Our salvation is certain and real. Hell is also very real. The suicide, however, either does not believe in hell, or he or she actually considers hell better than their present life.

It is difficult to understand why Christians would choose suicide. Don't they know they could go to hell? Perhaps they don't care. Their life is so unbearable. It would be easier to understand if we knew that they really didn't feel they would not be saved; that they hoped God would understand why they killed themselves; that they believed God would know their pain was too much to bear.

No one knows exactly how a suicide victim perceives death and/or hell. We do know one characteristic that could cause them to block out any thought of eternal damnation. This characteristic is called tunnel vision. It blinds them from seeing or using any other options to relieve their pain. Suicide is seen as the only solution for them.

As tunnel vision progresses they begin to need their thoughts of suicide to survive. They think and talk about death and suicide all the time. They are overwhelmed by suicidal thoughts and comforted by them at the very same time. They feel that if things get too bad they can always commit suicide and escape. Suicide actually becomes their light at the end of the tunnel.

Tunnel vision does not allow a suicidal person to listen to another person. The potential suicide could be told over and over again, "You're going to hell if you commit suicide," but it's likely that person does not comprehend or even care about what is being said. That doesn't mean Christians should not lay the facts of salvation and damnation on the line for potential suicides. They need to fully realize the possibility that if they take their own lives they could suffer eternal damnation for their lack of faith. However explanations of salvation and damnation may have little effect on a person with tunnel vision and suffering the pains of suicidal thoughts and tendencies.

Often suicides do not have contact with other people. They voluntarily cut themselves off from others. At first it may be simply not caring to be with other people. Soon they become afraid to be with other people. Being with other people intrudes upon the time they can devote to thinking about death. They also spend a great deal of time thinking about themselves. They dwell on their problems way out of proportion to the time spent on solutions. They think about how worthless they must be. They turn themselves into people no one likes. They become someone they themselves don't like. This person is not real.

Christians are to think about what Christ has done for them Paul writes in chapter 12 of Romans. Thinking about ourselves and our problems is bound to bring us down. Knowing that Christ died on the cross for us brings us up. Christ's saving act proves we are worth a great deal.

Consequently we should not measure our worth by how we feel about ourselves. For we are sinners doomed to hell. But we need to measure our worth according to how God feels about us. Through Christ, God sees us as perfect.

God has also given each of us very special and valuable gifts. We all have a purpose, and we are all part of God's plan. Romans, chapter 12 spells out in detail what the Christian life should be. We are told how to treat those who mistreat us. We are told how to work and act and think. Christians are not to pay back evil with evil. We are not to quarrel but live in peace with everyone as much as possible. Revenge is something to be left up to God. If we have enemies, they should be treated with kindness. By doing good we will make those who do us harm ashamed of themselves. Conquer evil with good.

Now take Romans 12 and apply it to someone with suicidal thoughts and tendencies. This person feels a deep and abiding worthlessness. He or she has measured value against the human self. Without Christ the human self is worthless. Christ gives a suicidal person self-worth. Christ is the only one who can cure suicidal thoughts and tendencies. Once a person believes in Christ and feels valuable that same person also has a special purpose.

Often the suicidal person has placed great emphasis on what the world expects. Doing certain things will establish a person's value and worth. So people are out there trying to become people God did not create them to be. They think it's important to do and accomplish things God does not want them to be involved in. When we try to do things God did not plan, we are suddenly out of our league.

We may become tired and frustrated. We may fail and begin to feel badly about what we are doing. We will also feel badly about ourselves. We will feel like failures. Some of us will change our ways and return to God's plan for our lives. Others will continue on the road of uncertainty and unhappiness. Anyone on that road for too long will likely feel suicide preferable to a totally destructive and worthless life on earth.

All of this can happen to a person very quickly. The person doesn't see or feel it happening. Friends and family members may see a change but not consider it a sign of suicide, especially where adolescents are concerned.

It is certainly not uncommon for teenagers to become less talkative and to spend more time in their room. Remember adolescence is a time when teenagers spend a lot of time thinking and planning their lives. They need time alone. So it's easy for an adolescent to become antisocial or suicidal without anyone noticing.

That is why it is important for parents and guardians to be in communication with their teenagers. We have to know more about what our teenagers are thinking. If we don't know, then we need to take the time to ask some questions. But it is wrong to say that communication needs to begin with our teenagers. Communication can start in the teen years. In fact it should start then if it was never begun before. Ideally though communication should be from little on with all our children.

It is very important for parents to know that communication is a necessary and vital part of childhood. The Bible speaks of childhood education in Proverbs 22:6, "Train a child in the way he should go, and when he is old he will not turn from it."

Communication is a type of education. We need to teach our children to communicate. We need to let them know they can come and talk to us. From very little on we should be letting them know that what they have to say is important to us. Parents need to learn to listen.

Listening to a child's endless chattering may almost be more than any human being can bear. However each time we take time to listen and try to understand we are telling that child he or she is worth listening to. If we do not learn to listen to our children when they are small, we will never hear what they are saying later on.

Parents who have not taught themselves and their children to communicate will find it hard to begin with adolescents. It is not impossible, however. The first step to take is to find a special time to be with your teenager individually and as a family.

A once-a-week meal out is an easy way to begin a relationship with a child or teenager. It is a time alone, and it also makes them feel important and loved by you. Each child in your family should have some opportunity to be alone with one or both parents every week.

Family devotions are the perfect time for sharing and growing together. Having devotions at the same time every day allows for daily contact. The contents of family devotions bring about discussion and almost always answer a question or solve a problem for one or all members of the family. That is simply how reading God's Word works in our lives.

Weekly church attendance lends stability to the family. It gives support for each member through regular contact with God's Word for comfort and guidance. It also allows each member to become familiar with the church and with Christian fellowship. Children will know where to go for help in their times of trouble or indecision.

Parents themselves can be examples of communication. If parents speak openly and honestly, so will their children. Likewise, if parents turn to God in prayer during times of trouble, that is where their children will go.

Parents can communicate their faith through their individual and family actions. If they are reading and studying the Bible, so will their children. If they are telling their children what they have learned, their children will share what they know about life and ask questions about what they need to learn.

Parenting is a very important job. Although it often proves to be more difficult or serious during adolescence, it does not begin then. Parenting beings the first time a newborn baby cries. By the time adolescence arrives, parenting is almost over. Teenagers can be allowed to go out and show the world what they have learned.

One look at the Christian family would seem to give us the perfect solution to preventing teenage suicide. One overwhelming problem of teenage suicides is the lack of self-worth displayed by its victims. A Christian family blossoms in self-worth, to say nothing of having a specific purpose and being a central part of God's plan.

Why then aren't Christian families the answer? It's a matter of statistics that children from Christian families commit suicide too. How could this happen? The answer is that Christian families also are made up of sinful human beings. They may pray continually, but they also sin continually. Because of sin things do not always go strictly according to God's plan. That is why Christian teenagers also have been known to take their own lives.

There is another important factor about suicide that parents and especially Christian parents need to be aware of. Suicide is a choice made by one person. It is not the choice of another, and no one including the suicide victim can blame anyone else for suicide. Only one person is guilty of suicide, the victim. The choice of suicide is made by one person, and one person will have to pay the consequences.

Parents are responsible to do all that they can for their children. Children are gifts from God. We need to know and communicate with our children. Parents need to be aware of and to try to understand the problems of their teenagers. However the ultimate decisions they make in life are indeed their own decisions. We ought not burden ourselves with guilt over another person's decision.

We can teach our children self-worth by letting them know how important they are to God and to us. We can also show them self-worth. Self-worth can be handed down from generation to generation. If parents feel self-worth, their offspring will be able to tell. If parents are and feel valuable, children will feel valuable. Likewise if parents feel happy inside, their children will know it. If parents are unhappy or always complaining, children and especially teenagers will pick up on unhappiness aspects of life and dwell on them.

Sad to say our teenagers are living in a complaining society. We complain about our leaders. It's hard to go out to lunch and not complain about our jobs or our bosses. Women complain about inequality. Men complain about too little pay and too much responsibility.

This is not to say complaining began with our generation. The children of Israel were noted for their complaining. When we read their story in the Bible, we can see exactly where their complaining got them, usually into a great deal of trouble. Down through the ages we have been programmed to complain. The old saying, "We're not happy unless we are complaining," still holds true today. This does not make complaining all right. Complaining is a sin, and it gets us in a lot of trouble with God.

A world where suicide is the second leading cause of death among teenagers is in a period of trouble. That God and his word are missing from the lives and families of so many teenagers compounds the trouble. Then the fact so many aren't aware of the trouble makes the situation catastrophic.

We could sit back and say the whole situation is too big and dangerous for us to handle. It is pretty big, and it certainly has become dangerous. Yet sitting back and doing nothing is not the answer. We can make a difference with the help of God.

The problem seems to center around what people have done in the past. The solution needs to center around what God can and will do in the future. God can change the hearts and minds of people — of those who want the biggest and the best; of those who place their self-worth on the same line with what they can accomplish; of those who have failed to accomplish anything and are thinking of suicide. God can change them all.

Some answers lie in St. Paul's letter to the Philippi- ans. It was a letter Paul was inspired to write to the Christians in Philippi while he was a prisoner in Rome. Paul had also been imprisoned in Philippi. Read Philippians 1:30 and Acts 16:19-40. Paul was surely no stranger to conflict and pain.

Paul had plenty of reasons to feel down and out. He could have even blamed God for his situation. He certainly had enough time to sit and think about all the bad things that were happening to him. But he didn't. Paul wrote this letter from prison. The keynote of his letter is: "I rejoice. Do you rejoice?"

Where in the world did Paul ever find even the slightest desire to rejoice? There is only one possession that would allow anyone to rejoice in such suffering, and Paul had it. He had Christ. He had faith and trust in God. His knowledge of God's grace made Paul joyous and content whatever his circumstances. Read Philippians 4:11-13.

Paul considered his joys greater than his sufferings. He considered his work for the Lord more important, more necessary and more valuable than any other aspect of his life. Paul did not look to himself, to his own life, but he looked to Christ.

Paul knew what his purpose in life was. Paul was intimately familiar with and understood God's plan of salvation. He knew the urgency of sharing the gospel. He realized that people would go to eternal damnation unless they heard the gospel. There was nothing more important to Paul than his Savior and his desire to share his faith in Christ. Consequently Paul did not have time to think of himself or of his sorry circumstances. There was work to be done, God's work! Paul was filled with joy at the prospect of bringing another soul to Christ. Paul was concerned for others. He rejoiced, but he also wanted them to rejoice, to be happy too.

We can certainly take many examples for our own lives from the Apostle Paul. When we get hung up on the problems of this world, we are missing the very reason and purpose for which we are here. Christians may forget the urgency and importance of spreading the gospel until they read again Paul's letter to the Philippians. He was not concerned about getting out of prison. Paul only wrote about one thing. He proclaimed Christ as Savior.

It is one thing for Christians to know this and practice this in their own lives. It is quite another matter to relate this release from pain and suffering through faith to a suicidal teenager. The sad facts are that Christians have brought the message of Christ and his gospel to suicidal teenagers. They have not listened. They have not been helped. They have committed suicide anyway.

Do these facts give us the right to stop proclaiming Christ to suicidal teenagers? Statistics may show that some teenagers who have been given the opportunity and training of Christianity have killed themselves. Statistics do not show how many teenagers have heard the message of their salvation — the story of God's great love for them — and have been prevented from taking their own lives.

Christians and the Christian message can make a difference. It's important to remember too that what we say is important but so is what we do. Adolescence is a stage of growing and learning. Teenagers grow and learn by watching adults. Teenagers are watching what we say and do. They are developing and planning their faith and lives by what they see and hear. If ever adults are called upon to be witnesses for Christ, it is with teenagers in the time of adolescence.

If we are happy, then let's show our teenagers how happy we are. If we are content, then let the world see why we are content. It is through and in Christ that Christians find happiness and contentment. This brings to mind a recent analogy that goes like this, "If you are a Christian, even your dog should know it." As Christians we see how much the world needs the message of Christian principles and especially of Christian faith. We can bear witness to the fact that Christ has changed our lives and has granted us peace.

Christians cannot cure the teenage suicide epidemic by themselves. We need God's help and guidance. With God's help we can begin to care for and prevent suicide among our teenagers. But we need to start with entire families. Let's tell them of Christ and how important he is to the world we know today. We can show them through our lives that truly he is the answer. Let's give of our lives so that teenagers will no longer have to be growing up all alone.

Five
Facts and Fallacies

By now you have become more familiar with teen-age suicide — what causes it and what can be done to prevent it. To help further your study of suicide, you may want to take the True or False quiz that follows. Try to determine in your own mind which statements are true and which are false. You may mark them in the book for future reference.

— Someone who talks about suicide will not attempt it.
— Someone who attempts suicide unsuccessfully will never try it again.
— A depressed person who suddenly appears happy and well-adjusted will not attempt suicide.
— People who attempt suicide are mentally ill.

- Suicide is biologically inherited.
- Suicide is contagious.
- Suicide occurs mostly among the very rich and very poor.
- The weather does not cause suicide.
- Most suicides happen in the winter.
- Most suicides occur at night.
- Suicides always leave notes.

For one reason or another all these statements turn out to be false. Let's begin with the first statement. Will someone who talks about suicide actually attempt it? The answer of course is Yes. A person may be simply asking a lot of questions about suicide. But a person also may use suicide threats to control the people around him or her.

The person who asks questions needs answers. Some people think as long as they give answers and keep the lines of communication open there can't be a threat of suicide. Just talking about suicide gives needed therapy. In some cases this may be true. Still, no one is qualified to judge which cases will commit suicide. So we must get professional help for anyone who is asking questions about suicide. We just don't know which cases are serious.

It is the same with persons continually threatening to take their own lives. They may be using suicide as a way to control the people around them. That does not eliminate the possiblity of them carrying out their threats. They too need help. People who talk about suicide do it.

Then there may be a person who makes statements like, "I'm going to kill myself!" or "You'll be sorry when I'm gone." Sometimes when people say these kinds of things, they're just being dramatic. Sometimes, though, they mean every word they say.

How can anyone know the difference between someone merely being dramatic or seriously contemplating suicide? It is very difficult to know exactly when a suicide situation becomes serious. That's why it's important to take every suicide implication seriously. This does not mean we get every person who has ever declared, "I'm going to kill myself!" to professional counseling. But we will listen to that person to see how many more times he or she talks about death. We will try to find out if there are other problems. We will let that person know that we are there to support and help them. We want them to know we will listen to them and try to understand.

Reaching out, listening and being available are really all a part of being a child of God. As we love God who first loved us, we also reach out and love others. Christainity can add a great deal to a world where people feel so alone and uncared for that they seek to take their own lives.

People who talk to us about suicide may be thinking about committing suicide. Studies have shown that over 80% of the people who kill themselves have talked about it previous to their suicide. Some therapists, in dealing with suicide cases, believe that talking about suicide is the single most recognizable sign that suicide may be about to occur.

But teenagers in general do not communicate with adults. They rebel, mistrust and even reject adults. And adults busy in today's world do not spend as much time as they ought to communicating with teenagers. Consequently teenagers who are talking about suicide are not being heard by adults who could help them. They do talk to their peers. However their peers have less knowledge than adults about suicide. They also have fewer resources to be of any help.

There is another very hard to swallow reason that teenagers do not come to adults or especially parents with their problems. Parents are usually too much a part of the problem to be part of the solution. When a problem arises in the life of an adolescent, the parents more often than not are seen as causing the problem.

Parents are viewed as causing problems when they say No or use other forms of discipline to keep an adolescent on the right path of life. Adolescents feel they no longer need their parents to keep them on the right path. Still when they are left alone with their lives, they suffer from loss of self-worth and self-identity.

It is really these contradictions in feelings and needs that cause the adolescent so much pain. However it is the lack of communication between parent and teenager that makes the whole situation so dangerous. Parents do not find out their teenagers are thinking about suicide until it is too late.

Parents, there are alternative methods of communicating with teenagers. Parents who cannot seem to communicate and speak openly with their teenagers can observe their teenagers. This should include how your teenager looks and feels and even dresses. It should also include knowing about or listening to your teenager's favorite music. It is simply a matter of observing and coming to know your teenager through how he or she acts or what music is being listened to.

Why listen to their music? Music affects the hearts and minds of individuals. If certain music causes parents to feel depressed, it could possibly be affecting their teenagers in the same way.

That's why it's important for teenagers to listen to uplifting music. There are beautiful pieces of Christian music available. Teenagers may argue that Christian music is not the same as the rock music they like. Anyone who knows Christian rock music knows the music is very much the same. But the words are different!

So when parents listen to teenage music, they have to concentrate on the words. Anyone who has studied the words of some modern day rock songs has found some terrifying messages being brought to the ears of young listeners. Some songs go so far as to call on the power of Satan. Others bring an evil message to kill and destroy. The wrong kind of music could be a sign of a teenager's intent to commit suicide. It could possibly be the cause of a teenager killing him or herself.

Some teenagers may not be affected by the music they listen to. Some teenagers handle difficult problems that lead other teenagers to commit suicide. The point is that listening to the music of teenagers is a way of observation. If there are problems, signs of depression or the like, it may be time to visit your local Christian bookstore and look into some Christian music.

Another way parents can learn more about their teenagers is by observing what they watch on television. Parents could also find out what movies they are going to see. This knowledge helps parents to see whom their teenagers identify with.

The same is true of observing what a teenager may be reading or writing. Many suicide victims have been reading or writing about death for months before their suicides. Some have given detailed descriptions of their own suicides. Sad to say it is usually discovered after their deaths.

Cases have been reported of teenagers placing their diaries around the house in places where someone was sure to see them. Mothers have commented about being annoyed by the diary always lying around. After these teenagers committed suicide, the mothers took time to read their diaries. They found the record of feelings and pains that caused the suicide. There was the warning that suicide was coming.

Why didn't the parents read the diaries? Some parents were too busy. In most cases, though, reading another person's diary was simply not acceptable. It's an invasion of privacy.

Parents who are concerned about their teenagers for one reason or another should not go searching for diaries to read. This invasion of privacy may cause more problems than it could ever solve. However if parents find a diary or other written material lying around day after day, there may be something there that needs to be read and taken seriously.

Parents can also observe whether their teenagers appear to be depressed. How do we know if someone is depressed? Depression is most often present when extreme changes in eating and sleeping habits occur. A depressed person cries over little things or for no apparent reason. Depression often makes a person unable to make decisions. Unhappy teenagers often display signs of depression. So depression is something parents should watch for as they observe their teenagers.

Low self-esteem is considered the chief underlying cause of suicide. How can a parent know a teenager has low self-esteem? One type is a person who constantly puts herself down. This is a display of low self-esteem. If a person considers every challenging situation hopeless and if nothing you say or do ever makes that person feel better about life, that person has a low self-esteem.

Parents who observe low self-esteem in their teen-agers need to find ways to build them up. Find ways to compliment them. Show them your support. Be sin-cere, but never patronize your teenager. Be available to your teenager. Try to find some time to be alone with your teenager. Make him or her feel special and valuable.

Parents can also watch for sudden changes in behav-ior, such as from introvert to extrovert. Someone who likes to stay in their room or at home suddenly goes out on the town. Or an active teenager suddenly con-fines himself to his room. Parents may also observe a sudden disinterest in a hobby. A boy will no longer participate in sports. A girl will give up horseback riding. Even a sudden change in grades or loss of interest in school work could say something to a par-ent.

Another observation that always comes to mind after a suicide has been committed is that the victim put his or her things in order. An adult will have put business papers in order, settled accounts or arranged legal affairs. A teenager will place the contents of his or her room in a certain order. He or she may begin to give certain treasured objects away to siblings or close friends.

That the suicide victim made an effort to say good-bye is usually observed after the act also. The friends of the suicide get together and talk about the last time they saw the victim alive. They find that a systematic effort was made to contact each person who meant something to the victim. They usually had a wonder-ful last visit.

Observing teenagers to find out if they are using drugs or alcohol is important in itself. However where teenage suicide is concerned, it becomes a matter of life or death. Drug and alcohol abuse has been known to cause suicidal thoughts and tendencies. Once drugs and alcohol are removed from potential suicides, they improve and sometimes never feel suicidal again. Parents who observe their teenagers using drugs or alcohol and do something to help may be saving them from more than addiction. Both suicide and addiction are deadly!

There are many ways for parents to be in communication with their teenagers. If talking doesn't work, try observing. You may find out exactly what you need to save his or her life. Remember teenagers may not verbally express their thoughts about suicide. They can and do communicate through how they look and dress, what they listen to, and what they are or are not involved in. So people who talk or communicate about suicide will attempt suicide.

How about those who attempt suicide, do not succeed, but live on. Will they try suicide again? Or will they be too ashamed?

The person who attempts suicide usually has reached the lowest point in his or her life. He no longer feels a desire to live, or in a sense she is ashamed of her life. The failure at suicide adds to that shame. It makes life even more unbearable. This person will likely try suicide again. Shame does not prevent suicide; it is one of the causes.

Some people who attempt suicide find out they really don't want to die. They are sorry for what they did. They thank God for sparing them. They probably will not try suicide again.

Another fallacy is somewhat ironic. A person who has been depressed and on the verge of suicide suddenly appears completely calm and content. This person is a high risk for suicide. Sudden improvement can be followed by suicide in a few days, a few weeks or a few months. This is what makes suicide so hard to prevent. A person can be gradually improving after hospitalization, or even be in a hospital, and still attempt suicide.

Why do depressed persons who suddenly seem happy attempt suicide? Because they have finally found the answer to all their problems. That answer, of course, is suicide. Once a person sees there is an end or a solution to pain or problems, he or she usually can endure. It is the same with a suicide. It may take weeks or months to plan just how to commit suicide. Once the decision is made to do it, there is a sense of relief and an appearance of happiness.

Here is where Christianity can have it's strongest influence. Christ promises an end to all pain and suffering. Christ again becomes the One to help a suicide find relief and happiness. In Christ the potential suicide finds hope for the future and no longer plans to die but to live.

People who attempt suicide are not necessarily mentally ill. There are people whose mental illness causes them to take their own lives. They are the most difficult if not hopeless to work with. One way or another they will take their own lives. But the mentally ill are not the majority of people who attempt suicide. Most are everyday people who have been overwhelmed by everyday problems. Especially is this true of teenage suicides.

People who are helped through the crisis period, the time when suicide is actually attempted, more often than not never attempt suicide again. It is not an on-going mental problem for them. It is a moment, a split second, when they couldn't cope.

This fallacy of suicides being mentally ill goes hand in hand with the fallacy about suicidal tendencies being inherited. Suicide is not biologically inherited, that is, passed from generation to generation through genes.

People choose suicide to solve their problems. If a mother chooses suicide to solve her problems, a child may also choose the same method of problem solving. The mother doesn't pass suicide on biologically, maybe emotionally. The child does not inherit suicide, but chooses suicide.

Neither is suicide contagious in the sense that you can catch it from being around suicidal people. No one catches suicide, they choose suicide. Still it's true teenage suicides often come in clusters. One teenager commits suicide, and others seem to follow. This does not happen because suicide is a contagious disease. It happens because one teenager used suicide to solve one problem.

Many teenagers have the same problems. They are desperately seeking solutions to their problems. If they see another teenager using suicide to solve his problems, they simply follow the leader. Same problem, same solution, suicide.

Our studies so far show definitely that suicide cannot be said to occur mostly among either the rich or the poor. Suicide can be attempted by anyone regardless of race, sex or socio-economic position.

It is interesting to note what part the weather seems to play in suicide attempts. At first we would guess that stormy, cloudy or cold days would bring someone thinking of suicide to attempting it. However the opposite is true. Potential suicides can cope with their feelings more easily when the weather is depressing. They cannot tolerate bright, sunny days, and so that is when most suicides occur.

Likewise we might guess that winter, a dreary time, is when people thinking about suicide might attempt it. But spring seems to bring on more suicide attempts than other seasons of the year. Spring is a time of newness of life. Suicides can't cope with new life. It clouds the view of death they find so comforting.

Most suicides do not occur at night. The darkness seems to shield the victim from the reality of problems and pain. But facing a new day drives a victim over the edge to suicide.

Finally, few victims leave suicide notes. Some coroners will not declare a death suicide unless a note has been found. This is usually done to spare the family the truth. In effect denying or avoiding a death by suicide verdict spares the family little or nothing.

The question that devastates a suicide's surviving family and friends most is Why? Why did the suicide happen? A suicide note gives the family some idea of the problems faced by the victim.

Without a note the mourners will probably never know why the suicide happened. If the suicide is denied, they will not even be allowed to ask why. Any despair they feel will be kept inside to fester and grow.

The verdict of suicide cannot and should not be determined by whether or not a note has been found. If suicide is evident, it needs to be dealt with by family and friends. Specific ways Christians can care for suicide survivors are suggested in the last chapter of this book.

Before we begin to think about how Christians can care for suicide survivors, we need to be thinking of ways to care for persons before they become suicide victims. In order to do this we need to be aware of resources that will help us and help them.

Suicide is indeed a crisis. There are crisis counseling centers and hotlines in all fifty states and Canada. They have anonymous, confidential, over-the-phone counselors. To find them, check the telephone Yellow Pages under *Suicide* or *Crisis*. Check the front of the telephone directory for the list of community services. Call a hospital emergency room. If they can't help, they will refer you to a crisis center. Larger hospitals will let you speak with a psychiatric counselor on the phone.

For more information on suicide write to: The Samaritans, 500 Commonwealth Avenue, Boston MA 02215; The National Institute of Mental Health, 5600 Fishers Lane, Rockville MD 20857; or The American Association Suicidology, 2459 South Ash Street, Denver CO 80222.

Here are some immediate counseling aids and suggestions. If you suspect someone is thinking of suicide, ask them how they feel and why. Don't be afraid your questions will give the person the idea of committing suicide. Most depressed people already have thoughts of suicide. They will be relieved to be asked and will want to talk to you or someone.

If they refuse to open up to you, that is all you can do. You cannot force them to talk. You can pray for them and remain available to them. Don't feel guilty about not being able to help them. You have placed them in God's care by prayer. You cannot help them any more than that at present. Make sure they know the crisis counseling phone number. Let them know the name of a counselor. However if they do not open up to you, chances are they may not seek help elsewhere either.

If you know a person who is definitely suicidal, if that person has confided in you about committing suicide, if you happen upon that person attempting suicide, the following facts will be of tremendous help for you to know. Encourage the person to talk. You

80

will need to talk too, but most of all you will need to listen and to pray. Listen for and to the person's pain. Ask God to help you understand and to give you the words to say.

This will not be a time to condemn. You can share your faith in Christ and tell how Christ has helped you through some rough times. Do not promise that Christ will remove all pain and suffering. God can and does do that in some cases. There are times, also, that God in his wisdom allows suffering. The person must be made to feel God will help him or her through the suffering, but will not necessarily remove the pain.

Read 1 Corinthians 10:13. This is an excellent passage to use when troubles seem to be overwhelming. It gives the assurance that God will not give us more than we can handle with his help. This shows that suicide is not the answer to temptations, trials and troubles. Faith and trust in God are the answer.

As soon as possible you will want to get help for yourself and for the suicidal person. Call the crisis counseling center or a close friend. This is not something anyone should handle alone.

If help is slow in coming and you are facing an emergency situation, you will want to find out the motive and method for suicide. Find out specific causes why the person wants to commit suicide. Once you find out, you may be able to place the events in a more rational perspective for the person. You can suggest other alternatives to take away the pain these events have caused in the life and mind of the person. People on the verge of suicide do not think clearly. There is much to be said for someone who can sit down and help him or her sort things out logically.

Finding out the method can be just as important. People often have spent a great deal of time planning suicide. They have committed themselves to a specific method. For example, a person afraid of heights told her therapist, "I'd never jump off a high building. I'd be scared to death!" But she would not be afraid of taking an overdose of pills.

If you find out the method, and it may or may not be evident, you can possibly block the attempt. In any case a trained counselor will be very happy you know the method. This will help the counselor to more quickly help the potential suicide.

Once you have stopped the suicide attempt and gotten the person to safety and counseling, you will have some serious decisions to make about your involvement with the person in the future. If you inadvertently happened upon a suicide attempt, you would not have any substantial contact in the future, unless you choose to do so. They key word here is, of course, choice.

Dealing with someone who is suicidal is a difficult and demanding task. You may or may not wish to be involved. Some professionals may choose not to handle suicide cases because of the intensity of involvement and the measure of responsibility. If you are a friend of the suicidal person or a family member, your choice is somewhat limited. You will almost have to have minimal involvement. There will be help and counseling available for you as well as for the suicidal person.

There is also help for you in the Bible. For an example go to the story of Elijah in 1 Kings 19. Elijah had gotten into a lot of trouble with a very wicked queen named Jezebel. She had threatened to kill Elijah. Elijah ran for his life. He asked God to take his life rather than allow him to face the persecution by Jezebel. Elijah was a great prophet of God, yet Elijah ran in fear when his own life was threatened. God certainly had reason to be disappointed in Elijah. Surely such a man of faith should be able to place his life and trust in God. Instead Elijah was asking to die. What did God do? God did not condemn Elijah; he counseled Elijah. God sent an angel to give Elijah nourishment. Elijah was also allowed to sleep. He rested. Rest and nourishment are very important for people overwhelmed by problems.

Then God put Elijah to work. Elijah was to anoint a new king and find a new prophet to take his place. Elijah was not to sit around and contemplate his problems. There was work to be done, work for the Lord.

From Elijah's story we can see how working for the Lord can actually be a solution to our problems and especially to the problem of someone wanting to die. Christians are not to be idle, but about the Lord's work. "Idleness is the devil's workshop" is certainly true when working with potential suicides. They want to be alone to think about their problems and about death. The more time they spend thinking about their problems the larger their problems become. The more time they spend thinking about death the more death seems to be the only solution.

Their problems are really no different or more difficult than someone else's problems. The world is full of people, and those people all have problems. Most people find ways to handle their problems, but others allow their problems to handle them.

There are many ways people can choose to handle their problems. There are many alternatives available. No one has ever been able to find out why some people can see only one alternative, suicide. There have been many studies done on suicide and recently on teenage suicide. So much more needs to be learned about how to help prevent suicide.

We've spent some time in discussing what concerned Christians *should do* to help in the care for potential and attempted suicides and in the prevention of suicide. There are also some things we *should not do*.

Do not promise to be a suicide's friend for life. You are placing yourself in a permanent relationship, and circumstances may not permit you to continue that relationship permanently. If the relationship is broken, suicide may occur, and you may carry guilt over the suicide.

Also, do not make deals with the suicide, such as, "I'll do anything you want as long as you promise not to commit suicide." You will be setting yourself up in a pressure pattern that you may have to break sometime. You will also be making yourself or your actions responsible for keeping that person alive. You will have your very own crisis situation if that person commits suicide in spite of all your efforts.

Lastly, do not feel guilty over someone else's choice to take his or her life. We can be caring and concerned. We can devote our time to helping someone who is suicidal. We cannot stop anyone from committing suicide if that person is determined to end it all.

Something deep inside has taken control and given the person determination to attempt suicide. Even the most loving family and friends cannot control a suicidal person. The fact is the person cannot control him or herself. When it comes to the death act, truly only God can stop suicide.

Well, then, why doesn't God stop suicide? The answer lies in our own free will. God created each and every one of us with our own free will. We do not live in a vacuum. God allows us to make our own choices.

The important thing to remember is that suicide is a choice. People choose it to solve their problems. Every person, every individual, is responsible before God for his or her choice. We will not be punished for anyone else's choice. We need not feel guilty for anyone else's choice.

Parents of teenage suicide victims are often filled with guilt over their son's or daughter's death. Chapter eight will deal with specific ways to care for suicide survivors. For now it is important to note that parents are not guilty of their child's choice to commit suicide.

This is why it's important, even in the case of attempted suicide, for the entire family to receive counseling. Whether the suicide attempt was successful or not, the entire family suffers. The entire family needs to be helped. Counseling can be difficult and painful. Parents who feel uneasy about their parenting abilities could feel threatened by the counseling situation.

It is not the intent of counseling to condemn problems or inadequacies. Counseling, and especially Christian counseling, is designed to solve and heal. Counseling takes mistakes and wrong deeds and tries to turn them around so they can no longer harm anyone, parents or child.

Again Christianity stands out as the answer to a family's counseling needs. A family of a suicide may have done things they feel contributed to the act. If they live in guilt from the suicide, they will not be able to live a normal happy life. The guilt could even overpower one or more of them. They could be plagued with emotional problems, even with another suicide.

If the family of a suicide is shown the forgiveness through Christ, any guilt they may feel will be eased. The family will be able to live in love and peace through the birth, death and resurrection of their Lord and Savior, Jesus Christ. They will even be able to handle all future problems and pains with God's help and guidance through his love, forgiveness and peace.

In this chapter we have dealt with fact and fallacy as well as some of the *do's* and *don't's* of dealing with suicide cases. We have come to an important realization — Christians can help in the prevention of teenage suicide and in the care of the survivors.

The next chapter will deal with the importance of knowing what suicide is and what suicide is not. This book is primarily for adults, who need to know more about teenage suicide. Hopefully adults will share what they learn with teenagers. Adults also need to understand the teenage peer group and how important this group is to the prevention of teenage suicide.

Six
Telling It Like It Is

What would you do if a very close friend started to talk about suicide? If you were the same age, in the same grade and in the same school, you might react in one of two ways.

One, you might no longer consider that person your friend. Let's face it, suicide is a morbid subject. Most people shy away from morbid subjects. You can't have a real close friendship with someone who suddenly turned morbid on you. If the person talked to you, maybe you would listen and try to at least be nice. On the other hand you could feel totally annoyed and avoid this person at all costs.

Two, you could try to remain friends out of loyalty if nothing else. You could listen to your friend's continual talk about suicide. Even if your friend calls you in the middle of the night to talk, you force yourself to listen. Your family may become upset with the midnight calls. You may even resent your friend's calls, but you still make yourself available. You try to say things to help your friend. You keep your friend's secret. Your friend has sworn you to silence. If anyone found out the two of you were talking about suicide, they'd probably think you both were crazy.

Now, which one of these reactions would be the better way to handle the situation? Neither reaction is better for you or for a friend thinking about suicide. Neither reaction will help you or your friend.

What should happen when one realizes a friend has suicidal thoughts? This chapter will deal with answers to that question. I hope those who read this chapter will share the answers found here with teenagers and their peer group.

First of all we will try to understand why teenagers who feel a close friend may be suicidal do not share that information with someone who can help. One reason is the same as an adult might give. They don't think the teenager's threat of suicide is actually serious.

Teenagers are young and alive. They have their whole lives ahead of them. Most of them appreciate their lives and look forward to living for a long time. Few teenagers die from illness or tragedy. Teenagers don't picture themselves as dead. They see themselves as indestructible. Few teenagers can even imagine the death of their best friend. Much less can they picture their friend taking his or her own life. "They may talk about it, but they would never actually do it," teenagers may say about their friends.

Another reason teenagers do not tell on their suicidal friends is that they have very limited resources. Whom could they tell? Many teenagers distrust adults, and that leads to serious problems in communication. It is important for teenagers to communicate with adults, but the fact is they do not. When a situation becomes desperate, some teenagers do go to school counselors. However teenagers may or may not consider a suicidal situation desperate enough to seek help.

There is one major reason why teenagers don't tell. They've been sworn to silence. A suicidal friend has confided a very deep, dark secret. It is expected that secrets are kept completely confidential between friends.

Why does a teenager who feels suicidal want the secret kept? For many of the same reasons suicidal adults keep their secret. They are afraid of condemnation. They fear the reaction of society will be unfavorable. They are right. Society condemns and has unfavorable reactions to suicide.

There is also the false belief that all potential suicides are mentally ill. A teenager who is suicidal may fear he or she will be locked away in a mental institution for life if anyone finds out. That fear intensifies suicidal thoughts and desires too.

Why do teenagers think these things about suicide? It all comes down to a lack of knowledge. Teenagers do not know there is help for those troubled by suicidal thoughts and tendencies. The knowledge just isn't available how to and why it is important to get help for suicidal persons.

A teenager who suspects a friend may be suicidal may confide this information to an adult. But the adult, lacking the proper helpful information, may react adversely or give wrong information. An adult may even choose not to believe the teenager. The suicidal friend will not be helped, and the informing teenager will probably not confide in an adult again.

In desperation a teenager may seek the help of a school counselor. How many counselors have the training and knowledge to deal with suicide? They certainly should have, and many do. There are some who don't know where to get help for a suicidal teenager.

Teenagers will not have adequate knowledge of available resources. Unless teenagers are informed of crisis counseling centers and hotline telephone numbers, they will never use them. Teenagers need to be informed and taught about the prevention of teenage suicide, not only for themselves but for their peers.

We have a somewhat different problem when teenagers are sworn to silence by suicidal friends. They have a confidence they feel a deep obligation and responsibility to keep. However education is the answer here too. The facts and fallacies about suicide should be presented to all teenagers. They need to know what suicide is and what suicide is not.

Suicide is death. Teenagers need to realize that if their friend attempts suicide, and succeeds, their friend will be dead.

Now, a suicidal friend can be very persuasive in his or her demand to keep things quiet. He may threaten loss of friendship. She may threaten to reveal another confidence. Some may even threaten immediate suicide if anyone finds out their secret. So a teenager may feel it important, even necessary, to keep a suicidal friend's secret, unless taught the facts.

The teenager who breaks a suicidal friend's confidence may lose a friend. The teenager may suffer for a past mistake revealed by that friend in revenge. The suicidal friend may even attempt suicide to get even. All these things could possibly happen if a teenager were to tell the truth about a suicidal friend.

What if a teenager did not tell someone that a friend was thinking about taking his or her own life? What if the friend went ahead and attempted suicide? Worse yet, what if the friend succeeded? What if the suicidal friend were dead and the teenager knew he or she had done nothing, absolutely nothing to help?

Teenagers do not ordinarily of their own accord think in terms of what if. They usually deal with life in respect to what is best for them at the time. With suicide teenagers must be taught the tragic consequences of keeping a confidence as opposed to saving a friend's life.

Teenagers need to understand the harsh reality that suicide is death. It is not a peaceful sleep. It is not an escape from suffering. Suicide is the ultimate in suffering for the victim. But suicide also causes the survivors to suffer for a long time because they fear the suicide victim is in hell. Maybe they could have prevented it.

The hope and certainty of heaven is not there for the suicide victim. No one can comfort the survivors with the certain knowledge that the victim is now free from suffering. Knowing that damnation is a real possibility has kept people from attempting suicide. It also may cause people to plan their suicide attempts so they won't die.

There are two more important facts teenagers and all people need to know about attempted suicide. One is that you may succeed, and you will be dead! The second is that you may not succeed, but you may be disfigured or disabled for the rest of your life.

For example, a suicide who tried unsuccessfully to electrocute himself now lives with both his arms gone. There are people who survived after jumping from high places in efforts to take their lives. They are presently living with brain damage, seizures, paralysis or various other disabilities.

Even less violent methods can have crippling effects on a person. Those who unsuccessfully use pills or drugs are left with severe liver damage. Shooting yourself is considered to be a foolproof method. Those who have used this foolproof method unsuccessfully are paralyzed, blind and deaf today.

Suicide attempts are more likely cries for help than outright death acts. The person doesn't want to die as much as he or she desires to be helped. People plan their suicide attempts so they will be saved and helped. However plans fail.

One woman planned her suicide down to the minute. The night before she made sure her downstairs neighbor would be home the next morning. She also planned for her maid to come as always at exactly 9:00 a.m. So three minutes before nine she began to seal all her windows with towels. She locked the door, turned on the gas and put her head down on the oven door. The maid arrived right on time. She was concerned and immediately went downstairs to get the key from the neighbor. The gas had put the neighbor to sleep, not fatally, but soundly. The maid rushed for help and soon had the police breaking down the apartment door. The suicidal woman had left a note with her doctor's name and telephone number. It was too late. She was dead. This woman did not intend to die, but to be rushed to the hospital and saved by her doctor. She felt a suicide attempt would make a difference in her life. Perhaps she wanted to be noticed or loved.

A suicide attempt is not a way to get noticed or loved. Sometimes the attempt may gain some sympathy. But in general people become very frustrated with suicidal friends and relatives. They become annoyed with frequent attempts and tend to disbelieve or dismiss the seriousness of the attempts. Some families have reported even feeling relieved when a suicide attempt is finally successful. Then they no longer have to go through the agony of one suicide attempt after another, or hear all that morbid talk of death and dying.

This leads us to the people who feel suicide is an act of love. If they kill themselves, no one will ever have to put up with them again. Teenagers are especially susceptible to this idea. They find their friends reject them, and their family thinks they're crazy. To spare everyone a lot of grief they take their own lives. Consciously or unconsciously they are punishing the people who reject or think badly of them. However they hide their resentment under the false identity of love. These suicides often leave notes telling their family and friends how much they love them. This causes the family and friends to feel guilty about not having helped the suicide victim more.

Teenagers also possess the belief that suicide is somehow romantic. Either it is viewed as a lover come to take them away from pain and suffering, or it is an act that two young lovers can commit together to immortalize their love, or it is a means of reuniting them with people they loved who have already died.

Suicide has nothing to do with love. It is an act of absolute selfishness. It is done by one person and for that person alone. Family and friends suffer greatly as a result of suicide. Some families are reported not to ever fully recover from that one act of a very selfish person.

No suicide can be defined as an act of love. It is an act of violence against self and against society. Suicide is murder. Suicide is killing the self along with all that self has to offer society.

In fact one suicide affects a larger segment of society. This is clearly seen in the rash of teenager suicides. When one teenager commits, suicide, it seems others follow. They may be teenagers fromt he same school or the same area. The teenagers may even know each other. However it has been reported that teenagers from other areas have heard about the one suicide through the news media, and they have committed suicide. Others follow them, and still others follow them. So a larger portion of society has been affected by one teenage suicide.

Teenagers who feel their suicide would affect only themselves need to realize that just isn't true. Suicide can and does affect many people, those we know and even those we do not know. If more teenagers were made to realize that one suicide could be the cause of others, it would be a huge step in the prevention of teenage suicides.

Before the colonization of America, England declared suicide a crime against society. Suicide victims' families were prosecuted. They stood to lose their land and everything they owned. Families suffered for what the victims did.

Suicide victims' families are no longer prosecuted. However they do still suffer the stigma of suicide as in past generations. Suicide victims' families feel ostracized by their community and even their friends.

It is interesting to note that early Greek and Roman society did not consider suicide a crime if it was approved by the courts. If someone wanted to commit suicide, they needed only approach the court and request permission. If the request was approved, the person could commit suicide without fear of recrimination for the family. Permission could be denied on the grounds that the person still had state or family responsibilities. Early civilizations knew about the responsibility people have to society. If a life was lost, so was whatever contribution that life might have made to society. Society still suffers loss from suicide.

Christians know that God created every human being for a purpose and according to his plan. When a suicide occurs, God's purpose and plan have been thwarted as far as that one very special human life is concerned.

Also when a Christian commits suicide, he or she is no longer able to spread the good news of the gospel. We have already discussed the very real possibility of a Christian who commits suicide not being saved. We must also understand that the people the suicide was to tell the story of salvation may not hear the message. These people may not go to heaven because the suicide was not there to bring them the message of salvation. So then Christians have some very real responsibilities to God and to others. These responsibilities cannot be left to others for God has given them to us. Suicide touches the lives of more people than anyone can imagine. It could even be said to touch the lives of people who haven't yet been born, who will not be saved because we were not around to pass on the message of salvation through Christ.

Along these same lines people have certain responsibilities to society in general. Everyone has the potential to contribute something to society. The contribution could be a life of service, recognized or unrecognized, or it could be suicide.

Suicide is passed from generation to generation. Parents can pass on suicidal thoughts and tendencies to their children, not biologically but emotionally. How many parents who choose suicide to solve their problems fully realize they may be responsible for a child of theirs committing suicide also?

One person may commit suicide, but many people stand to be hurt by it. Suicides may deny that they are hurting anyone but themselves. Christians can state the facts as they are and tell it like it is. If we can prevent one suicide by knowing and being able to present the facts, it will be worth our time and our effort.

There's yet another reason for informing a potential suicide of his or her responsibilities to God and to society. By making a person feel responsible, you are also making her feel needed. You are showing him his purpose and therefore his value and worth in life.

One might ask if adding responsibilities to the pressures already building up could cause a person to attempt suicide. Shockingly the answer is Yes. Giving the suicidal person the facts, telling it like it is, could bring about a suicide attempt by that person.

Could is the key word here. That's what makes suicide so difficult and dangerous to deal with. In dealing with suicide a person is taking that risk.

For the sake of clarification we will consider some alternative counseling for suicidal individuals. This need not be Christian. We send a suicidal person to a professional counselor. The counselor will help the person to go deep inside him or herself and get all the angers and all the problems out in the open.

Now consider the situation at this point. The suicidal person now realizes how angry he or she is and the problems he or she has. He or she may even know whom to blame for all the anger and problems. This knowledge could overwhelm the individual and cause an attempt at suicide.

We have to realize suicide could occur no matter what counsel and help is given to the individual. Suicide is viewed as a solution, a choice, by the victim.

Suicide is not necessarily caused by problems. It is caused by people who use it to solve their problems, or so they think.

Every person living on this earth today has problems. Problems that drive some people to suicide cause other people to succeed in life. One person may allow depression to eat away at their very soul. Another person will stand up to depression, fight it and thereby become a stronger individual emotionally.

No guidelines have yet been established for why certain people react in certain ways. We know that they do. Each person is different. Christians believe God created each person different for some special reasons. We accept God's plan and try to live according to it.

In dealing with potential suicides we need to understand that we cannot in effect cause suicide. If we do something to offend a suicidal person, he or she does not automatically have to choose suicide. People offend people every minute of every day. Those offended do not go out and commit suicide, unless of course they choose to. Even if you have a very poor relationship with another person, your dislike will not cause a suicide. Perhaps you could have done something to prevent the suicide, but that in no way makes you responsible for the person's choice to die.

A case of malpractice against some Christian ministers recently went through the court system. The parents of a young suicide victim accused the ministers of malpractice in counseling. The parents blamed the ministers for heaping so much guilt on their son that he committed suicide. After hearing the case the judge realized the ministers did not want to cause a suicide. They had counseled the young man against committing suicide. The ministers were found not guilty.

In Christian counseling it is necessary to use the law. The law of God shows us our sin. Romans 7:7 says we wouldn't know we were sinning if we didn't have the law. If we do not see that we have sinned, we will not know we need forgiveness through Christ.

Suicidal persons need to be brought to the realization that suicide is wrong. It is a sin. Suicide is physical death and could very possibly be eternal damnation. Although these facts can cause a great deal of guilt, they are also the steps to forgiveness and salvation. These steps need to be taken.

The pathway to heaven is difficult. The Bible warns against succumbing to temptations which lead to death. But the Scriptures also promise blessing to the person who perseveres through trials. Read James 1:12-15.

Life is going to have problems and trials. God does not allow hard times because he wants us to commit suicide. God wants all people to be saved. Read 1 Timothy 2:4. He wants us to feel loved, for indeed he loves us very much.

God wants us to live in peace and hope. He does not want us to live depressing worthless lives. We do not deserve all that God in his mercy and grace offers us. We are all sinners. God loves us anyway. God saves us in spite of our sinfulness. Read Romans 5:8.

We don't have to consider ourselves worthy of God's love and forgiveness. He gives them to us freely by his grace. God chooses us; we do not choose him. Read John 15:16. And God gives us his peace. Read John 14:27.

Listen to this story. A young mother endured one tragic illness after another. Her children were literally brought up in a hospital waiting room. Needless to say this family had much they could have been depressed about. One Sunday the family was attending church together. The pastor based his sermon on 2 Corinthians 12:9. (Read!) This is the verse where God tells Paul that he will not remove Paul's suffering, but will give him the power to endure. God's promise was sure. We know that Paul did endure great suffering. We also know that he lived in and with a great sense of peace and joy.

The pastor made the important point that our own sufferings serve to strengthen us. The more sufferings we have, the more we need God. The more we need God, the more wonderful our lives become. Our lives abound in God's peace and joy. One daughter, upon hearing that sermon, wrote her mother this note: "Mother, you truly must be blessed with the most wonderful life of all."

This family did not view suffering as a reason to become depressed. They had come to know through God's Word that sufferings strengthen faith. When God allows suffering to enter our lives, we can feel honored. Or as the daughter so beautifully wrote to her suffering mother, we can feel blessed.

God offers each and every person who hears the gospel forgiveness through Jesus Christ. We need to be aware of that. God's forgiveness is offered. It is free for the asking. Read 1 John 1:9. Still we need to repent and confess. God will forgive.

One woman confided to a Christian friend that she had undergone an abortion to save her life. The recurring thoughts about the abortion were causing the woman to suffer grief and remorse. The Christian friend asked if the woman had gone to God in prayer and asked his forgiveness. "Oh, yes," the woman replied, "many, many times."

"Well, then," the Christian friend said, "Your sin now is not in having had the abortion, but in not accepting God's forgiveness."

How easy it is to get all wrapped up in sin and guilt. We think about it and dwell on the details. Pretty soon

we have blown it way out of proportion in our minds. But sin isn't trivial by any means. We need to be aware of our sins. Sin can overpower our lives. It can cause suffering. It causes death. But through Christ sin is forgiven. We have life if we accept God's free gift through his Son, Jesus Christ. Read Romans 6:23.

In Christian counseling of suicidal persons we are working with a great deal of guilt. We may need to intensify that feeling of guilt to get the facts out. The facts are important. They show how much we sin and how much we need God. They show suicide is wrong and God is the only answer.

The fact is that we are loved by God and that through Jesus Christ we can be forgiven, if we believe. The fact is that we can live in God's peace and joy.

The facts show what suicide is and what suicide is not. The facts are important for a person who feels suicidal to know. They are important for anyone to know who is dealing with a suicidal individual. These facts are especially important for teenagers to know and understand.

A teenager's peer group will be the most likely to know if that teenager is thinking about suicide. That's why it is so important that this group get the facts. A teenager often will tell a peer things he or she would not reveal to another living soul. The secret confidences shared by teenagers would most likely not be found out by any adult.

Often after a teenage suicide, the victim's close friends are questioned. In most cases these friends knew the victim was extremely disturbed, if not suicidal. These friends usually did not intentionally withhold help from the victim. They simply did not know they should get help.

One way for adults to help in the prevention of teenage suicides is to be in contact with teenagers and their peer group. If an adult is concerned about a certain teenager, it would be worthwhile to speak with that teenager's friends.

Of course talking to a teenager's friends does not mean they will immediately open up and tell all they know. Teenagers do not naturally trust or take a liking to adults. It takes time to establish a relationship helpful for both persons.

In taking time to establish a relationship with a teenager's friends you could run out of time. While you are trying to get more information on a teenager you are concerned about, that teenager could take his or her own life. So time is an element in teenage suicide. It happens without anyone knowing or suspecting it could happen. It also happens when someone suspects a problem but does not have the time to do anything about it. Suicide does not wait around. When time runs out, suicide happens.

The more people who know about suicide, the more help suicidal persons can have in dealing with their problems. Since teenagers are the most likely to know about potential teenage suicides, they are the group who need to know about suicide. This is the group adults must give the proper and helpful information about the prevention of teenage suicide.

How can we get teenagers all the information they need to know about suicide? By being available to them first of all. If you are reading this book, just sharing the information of this one chapter could make a difference for a teenager, especially one who is in contact with a potential suicide.

Other ways to get the information out are through local church and community groups. You could discuss the contents of this book with these groups. You could pass this book on to someone who could speak to and reach these groups. You could provide your local library with one or more copies of this book. The libraries have books about suicide. Very few of them deal with suicide, especially teenage suicide, in the context of our Christian faith and life. You could also place this book in church and school libraries. Talk to local pastors or librarians about obtaining a copy for their church or school library.

This book is about the prevention of suicide. Its intent is to stop suicide before it happens, before it is even thought of as a solution of a problem for teenagers or any person. It is also the intention of this book to provide the assurance of forgiveness and peace in Christ for those who are suffering overwhelming problems. This book wants these people to know that God is with them and that he will help and strengthen them through every trouble. Read Psalm 46:1.

This book teaches some valuable and important principles of Christianity. It emphasizes the strong need in today's society for Christian values, not only for adults and families, but especially as guides for teenagers. There is also the sincere hope and prayer that our children and our teenagers will no longer be left to grow up all alone.

Teenage suicide develops in a society which no longer places a high value on human life, a society where high morals have disintegrated. It's not because people don't care that their morals have reached a low ebb. Many people just don't realize things have actually become so harmful and life-threatening as they are.

Many people do not realize what is really happening with our teenagers today. They can't understand how teenagers could feel their lives are so horrible that they actually prefer to die. People wonder how a teenager could ever feel all alone in our crowded and busy world. How could a teenager feel so low when he or she has everything anyone could ever want or need? Teenagers who think about or attempt suicide do not have everything they want and need. At least they feel like they need more. Could that more they need be God?

As Christians we of course hope and pray that all people will come to want and need God. For teenagers living in today's society we see God and God's Word as a must, especially where teenage suicide is concerned. There is nothing we can give our teenagers today that will be more helpful than God's Word. There is no one who will be more supportive than God himself. He will always be available. God will always love. God will always grant peace and joy.

"May the God of peace, who through the blood of the eternal covenant brought back from the dead our Lord Jesus, that great Shepherd of the sheep, equip you with everything good for doing his will, and may he work in us what is pleasing to him, through Jesus Christ, to whom be glory for ever and ever. Amen" (Hebrews 13:20,21).

Seven
Handling Emotions

Emotions are a big problem where teenage suicide is concerned. Teenagers who are suicidal have let their emotions get out of hand. Emotions can make the tiniest problem into something so monstrous no ordinary person could ever handle it. That's why people need to be taught to control their emotions and place them before the throne of God. God can handle anything and everything.

God created people with emotions from the very beginning. The Bible tells us that everything God created he also declared to be "good". Read Genesis 1:31. So emotions were good, once upon a time. What happened to turn emotions against us? Sin entered the world. With the fall into sin emotions became sinful.

We know that God in his mercy did not leave us in our sins. He promised and sent a Savior to forgive our sins. Through the grace of God we now have the power to handle our emotions. Without God we can do nothing, but with God all things are possible.

Indeed, God helps us handle emotions. God created them to be good, and they can be good. Emotions are in fact necessary for life. Emotions can be good or bad, helpful or destructive. Emotions can make our lives meaningful or cause us to feel worthless. It's all a matter of how we handle them.

The Bible gives some very distinct guidelines for handling our emotions. Take, for instance, the emotion of love. The greatest commandment our Lord ever gave was to love. We are to love God and one another as God loves us through his Son, Jesus Christ. The Bible also shows us that love can be wrong if handled improperly. Loving money causes us to sin. Read 1 Timothy 6:10.

Fear is another emotion spoken of in the Bible. Fear is usually not a positive feeling. No one wants to be afraid. Yet the Bible declares, "Blessed are all who fear the Lord" (Psalm 128:1); and "The fear of the Lord is the beginning of wisdom" (Psalm 111:10).

So it is not the emotion that causes all the trouble. It is how a particular person perceives an emotion and handles that emotion. Teenagers need to be taught how to handle their emotions. The truth is most of us adults could use a refresher course too.

Even Christians too often forget that our emotions need not be handled by us all alone. We have God and his Word to help. God created emotions. He surely knows how to handle them. His Word gives guidance and strength. We do need to look to his Word. We cannot expect to just somehow know how to handle and to teach others to handle emotions.

We can first of all thank God for not just setting us on the earth without guidance or protection. It is a cruel and evil world out there. So God tells us to rely on his strength and his power and to be protected by his armor. Read Ephesians 6:10. God through the Holy Scriptures has given his beloved children a spiritual armor to protect them against their enemies. Even the ones we don't know or can't see.

Our enemies are indeed very powerful. They are not mere mortal beings of flesh and blood. Our enemies are the essence of destruction, the organized forces of evil itself. Read St. Paul's description in Ephesians 6:12.

We cannot withstand this evil alone; we need God's armor. God's armor is given to us through the death and resurrection of Jesus Christ. It defends us against the attacks of our spiritual enemies. Christ's victory over evil assures us of our victory in the battle against evil. Through God's Word we are equipped with the whole armor of God.

We need the whole armor of God too. One part of it is truth. Read Ephesians 6:14. Truth is important. For example, our judicial system is founded on truth. If the truth is not told, the entire system fails. Truth is desired by many but actually found by few.

Jesus spoke often of truth. It is an important element in our Christian faith. Truth is the very foundation of our Christian faith. The truth is that we are all sinners and unworthy to stand before God. Truth does not end there, however. The truth also is that God loved sinful and unworthy mankind. Out of that great love he sent a Savior. God sent his Son, "the way and the truth and the life" (John 14:6).

Read Ephesians 6:14 again. The breastplate of righteousness is the part of God's armor that clothes each believer in the robe of Christ's righteousness. Righteousness means right with God. Through Christ we have been declared holy, forgiven, righteous. That's a pretty strong breastplate. It allows us to stand without fear against attack and to remain standing firm in our faith forever.

Faith, then, is our shield. Read Ephesians 6:16. Medieval knights could be identified by the emblems on their shields. Likewise our faith identifies us as God's children. Our faith also protects us. With the shield of faith Christians can withstand all the trouble, all the trials and all the problems that come our way. All we need is to know, accept and trust in Jesus as our Lord and Redeemer.

For our feet God gives us a brand new pair of shoes labeled "the gospel of peace." Read Ephesians 6:15. Having a new pair of shoes makes us feel good. The gospel of peace assures us of the forgiveness of our sins and makes us feel brand new inside and out. When people feel good, renewed and forgiven, then they have peace, not a worldly peace, but a peace of the spirit. It can come to believers on earth when they place their lives and their trust in the Lord. It will definitely be there for all believers in heaven forevermore.

Another part of the armor God gives to Christians is the helmet of salvation. Read Ephesians 6:17. The helmet of salvation Paul writes about protects us against spiritual injury. We need the helmet of salvation for our eternal life as well as for our earthly life. Without its protection we could fall prey to the evil temptations of life and lose our salvation. Protected by the helmet of salvation we can know without a doubt that we will enter heaven. Whatever we suffer on earth will end, and we will enjoy heavenly bliss.

The sword is both an offensive and a defensive weapon. It can defend us against an attacker. It can also be used to attack an enemy. Read Ephesians 6:17 again. "The sword of the Spirit," Paul tells us, "is the word of God." The word of God was used by Christ to overcome the temptations of the devil in the wilderness. The word of God which Martin Luther writes about in his famous hymn, "A Mighty Fortress Is Our God," is our sure defense.

Truth, righteousness, the gospel of peace, faith, salvation and God's word make up the whole armor of God. These are what each and every Christian must put on to withstand the evil one and temptations. This armor of God is what concerned Christians have to offer the potential teenage suicide. Indeed this is what Christianity has to offer all people. For the teenager who is thinking about suicide this armor has special significance.

The teenager who feels suicide is the only answer to life's problems is fighting a losing battle. That teenager has given up, surrendered, waved the white flag. That teenager is ready to concede earthly failure and possibly eternal destruction.

Try to imagine yourself at such a low emotional state that you would take your chances in hell rather than live on earth one minute longer. In your imagination you have just barely touched on how a suicidal person feels deep inside. You may be able to feel how much a suicidal person needs God's love.

God's love is not extended only to those people who have their heads screwed on straight, or to those who have succeeded, or to those who have made contributions to society, or to those with loving families. God's love is extended to all people, even sinful people who desire to die. That's the truth! And we are protected by God's righteousness through his grace.

Now imagine a person who was naked and suddenly has been clothed. That kind of protection could give the needed strength and desire to go on a while longer and not to commit suicide. Imagine feeling warmer and protected. That's how a suicide who begins to place his or her trust in God will feel.

Even the tiniest flicker of faith can grow and grow and grow larger than any problem or insecurity. It will cover like a shield. By faith the suicidal person can accept the message of the gospel of peace. The gospel of peace reaches deep inside a person who is thinking about suicide, washes away old feelings of worthlessness and replaces them with new feelings of self-confidence, purpose and value in life. With the gospel of peace comes the knowledge of salvation. A suicidal person who believes in Jesus Christ will no longer want to die, but will know life both on earth and in heaven. It will not be a life of fear and pain but of joy and contentment. Fear and pain will never disappear until heavenly joy becomes ours. On earth Christians will encounter hardships, but Christ's love makes them bearable.

God's Word guides his children through all hardships and pain in life. Its strength downs the mightiest enemy, the devil. God's Word protects, strengthens and shows people how much they need God.

In sharing God's Word with potential teenage suicides we are offering them the protection and strength they need. So the whole armor of God becomes a key issue if not the whole solution to teenage suicide. But opening up your Bible and reading from Ephesians chapter six is not going to automatically stop someone from choosing suicide. Remember the armor of God is something each of us need to put on first.

God's armor comes in all sizes. God made every person different, but he made armor to fit them too. Some people don't feel like it fits. Remember suicide is a matter of how people feel. A suicidal person may come from a loving family. He or she may have a successful job or career. Still if he or she feels unloved or a failure, suicide often happens. So how do we go about getting suicidal people to feel like God's armor is for them? God wants them to have it, to be protected, to be saved.

There's no simple answer. Some people have hardened their hearts to God. We may find ourselves endlessly chipping away at a cement wall. One day we may break through and help another person. We may just break enough away so that when someone else begins to chip at their heart they will break through. The cement could be so hard no one will ever break through, and suicide could happen.

That's why putting on God's armor is important when dealing with suicide. It protects us from the remorse and guilt we may suffer if we lose someone to suicide. It also shows us we cannot work alone. We need God. It is God who will show us the way to break through the cement of hardened hearts. In the end it will be God who rescues the suicidal person, not any one of us. He can work through us to help those who need him. As we read various parts of the Bible, we will understand better how to help others. God will show us how to make each individual contemplating suicide feel that God's armor is offered to them and fits perfectly.

By reading the Bible we will come to a better knowledge and understanding of God. By studying the Bible we too can learn to handle our emotions. God's Word shows us how. By learning how to handle our own emotions we will be better able to teach others. We will need a solid foundation and understanding of the Scriptures to be able to counsel and help teenagers who want to commit suicide.

The important thing we need to know is that God is with us. We need not be alone in trying to help another person. God does not want us to work without him.

The potential teenage suicide needs to know and believe in God, and to feel he or she is loved and accepted and wanted by God. Read Matthew 11:28. Jesus asks us to come to him. He wants us to come to him. He invites the potential suicide to come to him.

The first step for this to happen may be for that person to be loved and accepted by you. When you love and accept a suicidal person, you also accept their feelings. You don't agree with their feelings. You simply accept their feelings as a part of the person you love.

Next, you need to deal with those feelings. You can show the person that feelings are all right if they are properly handled. But you must also show how feelings or emotions handled improperly are wrong and sinful.

The most important step, even if it isn't the first, is to show that person improperly handled feelings, wrong and sinful, can be forgiven. There needs to be a great deal of forgiveness involved in suicide counseling or in dealing with suicidal thoughts and tendencies within a family.

To forgive someone suicidal thoughts and tendencies does not mean you agree with him. But you listen to what he has to say. You try to understand how she feels and why she feels that way. You are not saying suicide is OK, but suicide is a sin, and I will help you see that with God's help. God can be a big help both to you and to the suicidal individual. He is always available. Anyone can approach him at anytime. He promises to hear and answer every prayer.

It is of course important to get a suicidal individual to professional counseling. A Christian counselor will bring God into the counseling process. However Christian counselors are not always available. That leaves you to bring God into the counseling. Your prayers for the suicidal person become very important in his or her recovery. Your Christian witness and the sharing of your faith become the foundation the suicidal person could build on.

When a suicidal person informs you there is no other way but suicide, you can offer another way —God's way. It is a way of inner peace and great joy and real contentment. It is a way of life here and of eternal life in heaven. It is available now!

When a suicidal person tells you no one has ever felt as low or like he or she does, you can share with them the story of Job from the Bible. The Book of Job shows a man at his lowest state physically and emotionally. God had allowed the devil to tempt Job. Job lost his entire family as well as all his possessions. Job did not keep his feelings to himself but shared them openly with God. The devil expected Job to turn from God in all of his trouble. Instead Job took his troubles to the Lord. Almost any suicidal person could relate in some way to Job and could then see how to handle problems.

What about the suicidal person who complains of having to handle the same problems, feelings and emotions over and over again? He or she finally just wants to give up. Having to go up and then down one more time is more than he can bear. She wants it all to be over for good.

Here the story of David in the Bible offers guidance. Read 1 Samuel 16-29; 2 Samuel 1-22. The truth is **114** David's life was a constant rollercoaster ride. He was happy as much as he was sad. God loved David dearly. He chose David for a very important purpose. David was the ancestor of Christ. God never gave up on David. God always helped David and loved him.

One has only to read from the Psalms in the Bible to know this was true. You will find David completely down and feeling rejected by the God he loves so dearly. Read Psalm 51. Then David will write of how he needs God for strength and guidance. Read Psalm 46. Suddenly in yet another Psalm David will rejoice in God's love and presence in his life. Read Psalm 23.

For the suicidal individuals who feel God does not expect them to continue in their pain, we have the Bible story of how God sent his one and only Son into our world to suffer great pain. We know Jesus did suffer for us. Jesus was a man too. That's important. He knows what human suffering is. Jesus did suffer and die on the cross for us. That is why we can now approach the Father sinless and guilt-free. Jesus died and rose again, conquering sin and Satan for us. We have the assurance that God loves us and will help us and be with us, no matter what life has handed us. With God's help we can handle our emotions.

We can handle loneliness. Loneliness is different than being alone. People may desire to be alone. Some people need a certain amount of time alone, especially to pray and be with God. A person may be alone a great deal of the time and not feel lonely.

On the other hand, a person in the middle of a large and happy party may feel lonely. This person may blame others for being uncaring. The truth is, however, this person desires to be alone. People are not reaching out to this person, but neither is this person reaching out to anyone else. This person has chosen to be alone and to feel lonely.

This is especially true in the case of suicidal persons. They develop antisocial behavior because they are afraid to be with people. They will shy away from a crowd. In a crowd they will remain mostly to themselves.

Being alone, then, is not bad unless we make it so. Unless we choose to handle it badly by feeling lonely. If we use the time we have alone to be with God, we will find our faith will increase, our life will be fuller, our joy more complete.

If we choose to allow the feeling of loneliness to overwhelm us and cause us pain, we may find ourselves thinking about suicide. This is the time when we need to recall from memory such Bible passages as, "The Lord himself goes before you and will be with you; he will never leave you nor forsake you. Do not be afraid; do not be discouraged." (Deuteronomy 31:8) and "Surely I am with you always, to the very end of the age" (Matthew 28:20). These passages assure us that God is with us; we are never alone.

God's Word does not stop with the admonition that we should never feel lonely. For those who have been overcome by loneliness he gives clear directives. In Romans 12:2-21 God gives a short self-examination for all Christians. We are to compare what we are doing to what we should be doing as children of God. We should think of others. If we spend our time thinking of how we can help or assist others, we will not be thinking about our own problems. We are to use the gifts God has given to each one of us. The lesson here is to look for our gifts from God. How often do we complain about gifts we don't have and don't recognize the many gifts God has given us?

Philippians 2:1-5 speaks to people having problems with other people. So many times we blame others for our own problems and troubles. There is really no one to blame but ourselves when it comes to how we feel or act. We can overcome our problems with God's help, or we can allow our problems to overcome us.

With God and his Word to help us, we also choose a Christian lifestyle. We think of others first. We recognize what gifts God has given to us and use them to his glory. We take responsibility for our choices.

In a life of love for God and one another we look to the Bible for guidance. Read 1 Corinthians 13. This describes selfless love or *agape*. This love leads to a life of complete joy and peace. It is a completely giving kind of love. We give up all the time we spend thinking and worrying about ourselves. We don't take time to feel sorry about our circumstances. *Agape* love frees a person to love God, others and even self. It is everything a suicidal person needs, if only he or she accepts and lives in this love.

Selfless love is very difficult for a suicidal person to accept. A suicidal individual feels he or she is the lowest form of life. Suicidal persons can't understand how anyone could want to love them; they don't even love themselves.

As a Christian, then, you can begin to work with a suicidal individual's sense of worthlessness and guilt. Finding out exactly why the person feels worthless is a key step. What deep guilt has caused the person to feel he or she is worthless? Here again the Bible is an excellent resource in dealing with potential or attempted suicide caused by guilt. All people sin. Read Romans 3:23. Every person is guilty of sin. Read 1 John 1:8. Everyone who repents and confesses, God forgives. Read 1 John 1:9.

The suicidal person needs to realize that God does not look at any sin as greater or less than another. To God sin is sin. When my sin is confessed, through Christ my sin is forgiven. I may choose not to accept forgiveness. I may choose to live in guilt. I may even choose suicide to try to escape.

It may happen that after people confess their sins they still feel guilty. This is a false feeling or emotion. It is not real but imagined. False or imagined feelings are prevelant among suicidal persons. How dangerous, no deadly, they can be!

It is very difficult to prove to a suicidal person that his or her feelings are imagined or false. Christians, however, are living proof that feelings about being unforgiven are false. A Christian confidently witnessing to his or her own forgiveness is a tremendously strong influence on a suicidal individual to prevent suicide.

Anger is another emotion that often gets out of hand. It, too, is not sinful in itself. There are times when anger is a necessary emotion. Anger, however, needs to be handled properly. Read Ephesians 4:26,27. When Cain was angry with his brother Abel, he killed his brother. Read Genesis 4:4-8. Anger that causes a person to kill is not being handled properly. Anger that causes suicide is not being handled at all.

Anger against self is a cause of suicide. It is therefore important that we know what God's Word has to say about such anger. Being angry is not always sinful. Christians do not lose their emotions, but their emotions should be purified. Sometimes we do things that are harmful to ourselves or others. We become angry with ourselves because of our actions. Because of our anger we try not to act in a harmful way again. This kind of anger is not sinful.

When anger is handled improperly, we try to punish ourselves for our actions. We refuse to forgive ourselves, and we won't allow God to forgive us. We deserve to be punished not saved, or so we feel.

The Bible tells us this is true too. We do deserve nothing but punishment. Still every single person who accepts God's forgiveness through faith in Jesus Christ will not be punished. This fact, this truth, suicidal individuals need to have placed before them over and over again.

God has taken a very personal interest in each one of us. He created us individually in his own image. Read Genesis 1:27. He planned every detail of our lives. Read Psalm 139:13-16. God knew our purpose even before he created us. Read Ephesians 2:10. Even after we ruined his plan, he loved us and sent his Son to save us. Read 1 John 4:9,10.

After all God has done for us, he does not want to lose us. He is on our side and wants us with him in heaven. All the anger in the world could not turn him against us. Unless we allow anger to take over in our hearts. Unless we choose to live in anger rather than in forgiveness and love.

The Bible tells us that Christ has chosen us. Read John 15:16. Yet there are people who reject Jesus, the Savior. These people choose to live in loneliness, guilt and anger. Their lives become so unbearable they simply want to die. So they try to kill themselves, and they sometimes succeed.

These are the people Christians need to reach with the message of true and lasting joy. This joy is accurately described in the Book of Philippians written by the Apostle Paul. Paul is an example for us of a person who could have choosen to live in loneliness, guilt and anger.

Paul was subjected to physical and emotional pain and suffering. He could have chosen suicide. Considering his circumstances there are those who would not have even blamed him. He didn't choose death; he chose life. Paul's life may have seemed tragic for those who don't know Christ. For Paul, though, his life was a glorious reflection of the God he knew intimately and loved dearly.

How wonderful it would be for a person contemplating suicide to come to know and love God, for a person overwhelmed by suffering and pain to know peace and joy. It can happen, and it has happened to Paul and many others. Now let's pray that it will happen in the lives of all teenagers troubled with thoughts of suicide today.

Eight
But, What If?

Sam Wirth was at the age where he didn't care to be called Sammy anymore. At 16 years of age and a sophomore at Denver Christian High School, Sam had a B-plus average, a varsity football letter, a prestigious reign as homecoming attendant and a brand new driver's license. He played a mean air guitar.

Five-foot-eleven, brown hair, blue eyes, Sam never left home without his comb. One week ago today, Sam Wirth killed himself.

This story was reported in the March 3, 1985, Denver *Post*. It was a tragic story. A story no one seemed to be able to understand. What possible reasons could a boy like Sam have for committing suicide?

The truth of the matter is that teenagers just like Sam are taking their lives every day in America. We have learned that there can be few signs of impending suicide and even less warning. We only know we need to be ready with some answers for our very troubled teenagers. We need to be available to them and ready to share our Christian faith and life with them. We must assure them that they are not growing up all alone.

Sam's story is not unusual in view of the many other teenagers just like him who have taken their own lives. But Sam's story is special in one way. That is why it was chosen for this book.

Sam, you see, professed to be a Christian. He attended a Christian high school. We know that didn't automatically make him a Christian. Sam wrote that he believed in God in his suicide note. Sam's note told his family how much he loved them and the Lord. He told them his life just wasn't working out. He felt like a failure. He apologized for what he was about to do.

The fact is that there was no apparent reason for Sam to commit suicide. The fact is that Sam said he believed in God. The fact is that Sam wrote he was sorry for what he was about to do. These facts should have stopped Sam from taking his own life. But they didn't.

When a suicide occurs, the question people want answered the most is Why? Why did the person commit suicide? Being able to know a little more about why aids in the grieving process that must follow the suicide act. If a suicide note was left, it may give some of the reasons. An analysis of the note will even allow for some reading between the lines. Any knowledge of why can be helpful to those close to the suicide victim. If no note can be found, it makes the suicide even more tragic. The question of why probably will never be answered. The victim's family and friends must live with a question that will come back to them over and over again during their lives.

In Sam's case there was reason to believe his older sister's death may have had something to do with his suicide. That was what the Denver *Post* reported. Sam's older sister Lorry died on Memorial Day in 1984, the victim of a horseback-riding accident. Lorry would have been twenty-five in February, three days before Sam's death.

Sam's parents reported that her death had haunted Sam. He wrote about it in a speech to his classmates that his mother saved. "And to this day I regret not showing my love to her as often as I could," Sam had scrawled on wideline notebook paper. "I think that it is so important now to show love to your family."

Perhaps Sam's suicide was caused by thoughts of his older sister's death. He apparently felt he had failed in not showing her love as often as he could have. He may have held the common misconception about suicide being a means of reuniting a person with a loved one already dead. No one will ever know for certain. Not knowing is the most devastating part of suicide for the survivors to handle.

So far we have learned a great deal about the prevention of teenage suicide. If we are aware of certain danger signs, we may be able to help someone through a suicide crisis period. Parents and adults in general need to take time to be with teenagers. The effects on teenage adolescents of being left to grow up all alone can actually cause teenage suicide.

No matter how prepared we may or may not be, suicide can and does happen. A teenager may have all the love and support of family and friends available, but he or she may not be able to feel that love and support. Consequently suicide happens. It is tragic. It is unexplainable. To some it is absurd even ridiculous. To others it is unforgiveable.

Suicide, when it occurs, can bring about many different feelings and reactions. Most of the feelings and reactions connected with suicide can be harmful and damaging to survivors.

First of all a feeling of guilt arises almost instantly. One person may blame another person for causing the suicide or not stopping it. Usually the person blaming another is covering up his or her own guilt. There is also the person who, directly or indirectly, consciously or unconsciously, blames him or herself for the suicide. Either he should have been able to stop the suicide, or perhaps it was caused by something she did.

This guilt is a false feeling. We need to remember that through Christ guilt is forgiven. So there is no cause for guilt if we ask to be forgiven. However in the case of suicide guilt is also false if it is felt by anyone but the victim. Suicide is a choice made by one person. That person and that person alone is responsible, to blame, or guilty of suicide.

If a person is unloved, there are many ways that person can deal with the particular problem without committing suicide. If a person is experiencing pain, there are many alternative ways of dealing with pain without having to resort to the taking of a human life. Suicide is not the fault of another person; it is the choice of the victim.

Suicide is really a matter of using, or should I say misusing or abusing, the free will all people were created with. God knew sin would ruin our world and his. That did not stop him from allowing us to find out for ourselves.

Adam and Eve quickly found out that sin is death. We would like to think that fact would cure us from ever wanting to sin again. Sin though does not work that way. The more we sin, the more we want to sin.

God sent his Son to give us the forgiveness of sins. His gracious gift shows that God still loves us. When someone loves you as much as God or does something for you as great as what God has done, you naturally desire to repay or to love in return. We know that we cannot repay God. We know that we cannot love him as much as he loves us. We want to try though. We do try, but when we fail, we sin. Our human nature causes us to sin. Our spiritual nature in and through Christ desires not to sin. These two natures are constantly at odds with each other. Read Romans 7:14-25. It is a spiritual battle that can only be won through faith in Christ. When the battle is lost, sin occurs.

It is important to point out that the battle could be lost by anyone at anytime. All people sin. All kinds of people fall into the temptation to commit suicide. As stated early in this book, virtually everyone thinks about suicide at some time in life. If a person is spared continued thoughts of suicide, is able to cope with various problems and pains in life, and does not commit suicide, it is by the grace of God.

In this chapter we are dealing with suicide survivors. Suicide survivors are the family and friends of a suicide victim. The victim is the person who has taken his or her own life by suicide. The suicide survivors suffer greatly from the act of the victim, and from the condemnation of society. It is the responsibility and privilege of Christians to help and comfort those who are suffering.

Although Christians realize their responsibilities and are thankful for their privileges, they seem somehow to believe suicide survivors are excluded from their help. Christians have been led to believe, through practice and tradition, that suicide is so great a sin that it even affects people who were close to a suicide victim. Suicide is indeed a damning sin. Anyone who commits suicide will go to hell if he or she did not repent. God will not judge the survivors for the act or choice of another. Neither should we.

Studies do show that comfort and support has been readily and willingly given to certain suicide survivors. These are the survivors or families who have displayed Christian lives. This is taken to prove to the community that the suicide was clearly not their fault. Christians also are less likely to condemn these families or survivors. However when a family has not been seen to be a caring unit or has not met certain community or church standards, that family stands a good chance to be condemned for the suicide of one of its members.

When dealing with suicide survivors Christians need to be in touch with their own feelings about suicide. What prejudices do we possess? What fears do we have about suicide? What facts about ourselves and our own sins would cause us to condemn a person for the suicide of another?

It is our Christian duty and responsibility to help and comfort suicide survivors. If we feel we cannot fulfill this Christian duty and responsibility, we need to discover why we cannot. Is it because we feel the survivors are as guilty as the victim? Do we fear being close to them will make suicide contagious or cause us to sin?

Whatever our reasons are for not wanting to help suicide survivors, they need to be dealt with. Christians cannot sit back and watch the suffering of suicide survivors and do nothing at all to comfort and help them. That would be sinful.

If Christians are to help and comfort suicide survivors, there are things we need to know. There are phases people go through in a grieving process. It is actually no different for suicide survivors.

The first phase in the grieving process is *shock*. Can we imagine the shock suicide imposes on anyone, especially a person close to the victim. If no one so much as expected the suicide, if none of the warning signs or danger signals seemed to be present, and if a suicide note was not left, imagine the shock of it all.

Christians in dealing with suicide survivors need to know that anything could happen during this phase. It is a tragic, terrifying phase. Even another suicide could happen at this point in the grieving process.

Relief is the second phase, but we would do well to realize it is sometimes hard to understand or even see. Some families may state that they are glad the victim is dead. They usually don't mean they are glad for the suicide's death. They feel glad they don't have to deal with suicide anymore. This feeling is usually present in a family which has had to deal with one suicide attempt after another. However it can certainly be present after even one successful attempt at suicide. Instead of condemning the family we should understand that this is a phase of grief. Any sign of considering the suicide over, no matter how morbid or uncaring the sign may appear, should be considered simply a part of the relief phase.

The most difficult phase of grief then follows. It is labeled *catharsis* or *cleansing*. This is when survivors try to get rid of any guilt they feel about the suicide. A survivor may blame him or herself for the suicide. Although this can and does happen in this phase, it probably will not be noticed until the next phase.

Behavior prevalent in the catharsis phase revolves around blaming other people for the suicide. The only way survivors seem to be able to get rid of their own guilt at this time is to give it to someone else. Survivors need to be led lovingly to a realization of what they are doing. Also they need to come to a full realization that no one is to blame for any suicide except the victim. Survivors who can't find anyone else to blame

for a suicide ultimately blame themselves.

This leads us to the next phase, *depression*. Remember that even people who blame other people for a suicide still feel guilty themselves. Almost every person close to or involved with a suicide victim feels some guilt or remorse. This will cause depression. We have learned that depression causes suicide. So we should be aware that suicide could occur again during this phase. Aside from that we need to know certain facts about how to handle depression.

First of all make certain the survivor(s) realize that depression is a phase of the grieving process. Have them recognize that it will pass. They also need to know that it is the most painful of all the phases and that it should lead them to confess their guilt. From our studies we know that survivors have no reason to consider themselves guilty. We also know that they do anyway. Remember we called this a false guilt.

Well false guilt can be just as damaging as real guilt. Therefore it must be dealt with. So the final phase is *confession*. People who feel false guilt need to confess their guilt. They need to get everything out in the open. They need to have someone explain to them, maybe over and over again, that their guilt is false. Some survivor families, especially if they are not used to communicating openly, never get to the confession phase. In Christianity, of course, if the survivor reaches confession, he or she is offered complete forgiveness and release from guilt.

If the final phase or any other phase of grief is not being reached by certain suicide survivors, there are reasons why. These reasons have been labeled "blocks." They are things that happen inside the suicide's surviving family or inside an individual that cause the grieving process to stop or slow down.

One such block is daydreaming. Daydreaming is not harmful all the time. Sometimes it's even fun. Daydreaming about the suicide victim can help a survivor accept the suicide and deal with it. But when daydreaming takes over the productive life of a survivor, it becomes dangerous. If a survivor wakes up in the morning and goes to bed at night daydreaming every minute of time away, the healing or grieving process is stopped.

Another dangerous block is preoccupation with the deceased. A survivor may think of the deceased occasionally. This is good and healthy. When the survivor beings to act and talk like the deceased, real problems have begun. Acting and talking like the deceased will not bring back the dead.

Dreams about the deceased are very normal. Accepting the dreams for what they are, just dreams, is important. Also knowing that the dreams are a part of the normal grieving process is very helpful to survivors.

If a survivor does not realize that dreams about the deceased or even about the suicide act are a normal healing process, the survivor could easily become overwhelmed and frightened by the dreams. The greater emphasis placed on the naturalness of these dreams, the sooner the dreams will disappear.

Shrine building is another block to discourage. Keeping a remembrance or two of the deceased may be necessary and certainly not wrong. However keeping the deceased's room just as it was as a permanent memorial causes the grieving process to go on and on.

Flashbacks are another block that can cause trauma if not handled properly. Flashbacks of the deceased and especially of the suicide act itself should be clearly

explained as absolutely normal. Given time they will become less frequent and then be gone.

Anger can become a large block for the suicide grieving process. Survivors tend to be angry at anyone and everyone. They are really angry at the victim for commiting the suicide in the first place. It's important to allow anger to come out as long as it doesn't cause harm or become a danger to self or others. What may be extremely harmful or dangerous to one person may hardly affect another. So anger is a very difficult block to deal with.

In dealing with anger Christians need to turn to God for the special strength and wisdom only he possesses and can give to his children. We need to know that God is with us and trust that he can work through even the angriest situation for good.

Any physical harm should not be allowed to enter the grieving process. Children or otherwise fragile human beings should be protected from angry remarks or physical abuse entirely. Angry words blurted out on a moment's notice with no particular meaning should be accepted as anger that needs to be expressed. Even anger at God should not be entirely off limits. God can take it, and God can forgive anger.

All of these blocks can severely hamper the grieving process. They should be watched and examined for their seriousness. They need to be explained to survivors and taken for what they are. If these blocks are accepted and understood, they usually come tumbling down. Most of these blocks will be found in one or two survivors.

There are some games entire families play that also prevent the completion of the grieving process. Scapegoating is a game played by suicide survivor families that blocks communication and healing. This game assigns the blame for the suicide especially on someone. It becomes necessary to somehow make the whole family realize that only one person is to blame. Only one person chose suicide, the victim.

There are families who attempt to keep the impossible secret. They know suicide happened — was committed, but refuse to admit what they know to anyone else. By keeping the suicide a secret they block any chance of healing for their family.

There are families who refuse to admit a suicide happened even when there are clear signs that it did occur. Some refuse to believe what is clearly written in a suicide note. If these families are not helped, they will not be healed.

There are families who form themselves into an every-member supportive system. They keep to themselves and fend off the rest of the world. They reject help and support which they desperately need. These families do not undergo any type of healing. Their feelings grow along with the barrier they place between themselves and help.

In some families one member steps out and takes the place of the deceased. Outwardly this seems to be the honorable thing to do. Inwardly it is often an effort to deny that the suicide victim is missed or needed. It blocks efforts to grieve for the victim. It also places unnecessary stress on the person trying to take the suicide victim's place.

Some families will decide not to discuss the suicide again verbally or even non-verbally. This is, of course, a way of denying the suicide ever happened and makes healing almost impossible.

Most families go through a phase where they decide which person was loved the most by the deceased. Then they place that person at the top of their list as their leader. It's a kind of honor they feel they must show in the victim's absence. This act is supposed to make up for the honor they did not show the victim in life.

This phase also reverses itself. The family picks out the person the deceased cared for the least. This person gains sympathy and sometimes power too. This family is angry. The members are trying to dishonor both the victim and the deed.

All these games are a means of directly stopping the grieving process. They freeze the action and therefore maintain the guilt and pain these families are feeling. Families who play these games have, whether they realize it or not, a desire to continue to grieve. They feel that by grieving they can somehow make up for the suicide.

If family members cannot rid themselves of the guilt and pain of suicide by playing games, they may choose to move away from where the suicide occurred. This is not all together unhealthy in view of the many reminders of the victim that could block the completion of the grieving process. However if a move is made in a conscious or unconscious effort to deny the suicide occurred, it is indeed unhealthy. Families who run away from the reality of suicide stand to suffer from that suicide for the rest of their lives.

Suicide and the effects it has on any and all survivors need to be dealt with. There probably aren't enough professional counselors to deal with all survivors suicide victims leave behind. It should be stressed though that as many as possible receive professional counseling and help.

This book gives only the basic symptoms and problems involved in dealing with suicide survivors. It by no means gives all the answers. Nor does it give any non-professional the license to do professional counseling.

Where suicide survivors need professional counseling, such counseling should be provided for them. It would be wonderful if that counseling would be done by a Christian counselor. However the prayers, comfort and support of a Christian friend can be a solid and beneficial addition to any counseling.

It's true that some counselors contradict Christian teachings and principles in their counseling of suicide survivors. If you see this happening, you may need to change counselors. Never use a certain counselor's poor practices or non-Christian counsel as a reason to try to do your own professional counseling. Continue to look and pray for the professional help and counsel suicide survivors need.

Christian care and counseling then comes in addition to professional counseling. At first look this may seem unnecessary. Once a family is receiving professional counseling, we think they no longer need our help. On the contrary! Professional counseling happens at most once a week. Sometimes it is as little as once a month. What happens to this family between those visits to their counselor?

Here is where Christians come in. Here is where we need to know about the grieving process suicide survivors go through. Here is where we must try to understand some of the blocks that cause the grieving process to stop. Only by knowing more about the needs of suicide survivors can we help and comfort them.

There is one final issue that needs to be covered in this book. It is the most difficult issue involved with suicide, but a very necessary issue. It has to do directly with Christians giving help and comfort to suicide survivors. The issue then is whether or not suicide is forgiven. No answer will completely comfort suicide survivors. When a person commits suicide, that person loses the certainty of salvation.

Now read Matthew 27:3-5; Acts 1:16-19; 2 Corinthians 7:10 and Matthew 26:75. Peter's grief was godly sorrow. This brings repentance that leads to salvation. The remorse of Judas was worldly sorrow that brings death. Consequently Judas becomes an example of a suicide being sorry, but not forgiven. That's what makes suicide so horrifying for its survivors. That's what makes helping and comforting suicide survivors so difficult.

First of all, there are often very few clues or even reasons why the suicide happened. Ideas about how the suicide victim felt or knowledge of the problems involved may help. A suicide note may give some explanations. Still the reasons will not be clear, and most often they are never even known.

Secondly, the eternal fate of the suicide victim is not definitely known. How often don't we hear that families have felt comfort in knowing that their loved one is with the Lord? Never can this be said of a suicide victim to his or her family. The suicide victim may have suffered intensely while alive. There is nothing that can assure the survivors that he or she is not suffering more intensely dead.

This hard fact will not allow Christians to adequately comfort suicide survivors. No matter how much they show their love and support, Christians cannot assure the survivors of the salvation of a suicide victim. Perhaps this is one reason Christians shy away from suicide survivors.

I hope that after reading this book Christians will not feel they cannot help when it comes to suicide. It's true the comfort of salvation in heaven cannot be there for the suicide victim or the survivors. This does not automatically negate the need to have salvation proclaimed.

Christians can look out into the world and see changes that are not pleasing to God. We can see clearly how these changes could very well ruin God's plan of salvation for many, many people. Already so many teenagers have lost their purpose in life. Christians dare never say or should never feel they cannot help.

Teenage suicide has reached epidemic proportion. Teenagers are growing up all alone in a world filled with problems they have not been taught to handle. God is turned to in crisis when it's too late. Christians can help. Christian teachings and principles are needed and necessary in just such a world as this.

This, of course, is the world we are living in. It was created by God, but it has been placed in our hands. Christians are not exactly in the majority. Christian teachings and principles are not practiced world-wide. But, what if they were?

What if God was placed first in your life exclusively? What if you would not allow anything to come between you and God? Not your job, your hobby, your relatives and friends, your church and community responsibilities? What if nothing could stop you from attending church every Sunday, reading your Bible every day, and praying continually?

Now what if you taught giving God priority to your children or a friend or relative? And then they shared what they learned about God's love and forgiveness, peace and salvation with others? What if more and more people would come to know Christ as their Savior and Lord?

Somewhere in the answers to these questions lies the answer to teenage suicide. As Christians we pray that our answers to these questions will be the right answers. With God's help our answers will be able to help in the prevention of teenage suicide and the care of suicide survivors.